VEGAN

30 Days of Vegan Recipes and Meal Plans for Increasing Your Health and Energy

Free membership into the Mastermind Self Development Group!

For a limited time, you can join the Mastermind Self Development Group for free! You will receive videos and articles from top authorities in self development as well as a special group only offers on new books and training programs. There will also be a monthly member only draw that gives you a chance to win any book from your Kindle wish list!

If you sign up through this link http://www.mastermindselfdevelopment.com/specialreport you will also get a special free report on the Wheel of Life. This report will give you a visual look at your current life and then take you through a series of exercises that will help you plan what your perfect life looks like. The workbook does not end there; we then take you through a process to help you plan how to achieve that perfect life. The process is very powerful and has the potential to change your life forever. Join the group now and start to change your life!

http://www.mastermindselfdevelopment.com/specialreport

Introduction

Veganism is fast catching up with many people across the world. The noble idea behind veganism such as not wanting to exploit the less fortunate animal species of the world by taking what is theirs and selfishly using it for ourselves simply because they do not have the power to stop us is, perhaps, the primary reason for the growth in popularity of this concept.

However, in addition to the above extremely thoughtful reason, the health benefits and other great things about veganism are all sufficiently powerful causes for the expansion of the idea of veganism across the planet. This book is written with an intention to exhort newcomers to try a one-month vegan challenge that has the power to change not just your lifestyle but your entire outlook on life.

Before you decide to try to change your lifestyle to vegan, there are a few things you must know and understand about it. This book aims to do exactly that by giving you a detailed overview in the following areas:

- What is veganism?
- A brief history on veganism
- How is veganism useful to you?
- Meal Plans for a one-month challenge along with recipe outlines
- How to stay committed to the cause?

What is veganism?

You know who are vegetarians? They do not consume poultry, meat, or, fish in their diet. Vegans, additionally, do not consume or use any animal products and/or by-products such as dairy products, honey, eggs, leather, silk, fur, and soaps and cosmetics made from animal sources. Vegans are the superset of vegetarians. All vegans are also vegetarians but all vegetarians need not be vegans.

Vegans believe that veganism is not just about their diet but a way of life. As far as possible, vegans avoid exploitation of animals in any form including but not limited to food, clothing, or other purposes. They also avoid items that have been tested on animals before being commercialized. And believe it or not, there is a vegan diet for all kinds of diets ranging from the junk food lovers to the raw food lovers and those in between, too.

History of Veganism

Veganism, although not known as veganism, has been around for many centuries. Examples of prevention of exploitation against and cruelty to animals have been written in history books. Lord Buddha of India and Pythagoras both advocated this concept and had put in rules to ensure their followers ate only plant-based food and completely avoided meats and animal products.

The earliest modern-day veganism is known to have occurred around 1806 CE. During that time, the great English poet P B Shelley and Dr. William Lambe publicly objected to consuming dairy products and eggs by humans on ethical grounds. This incident seems to have laid the foundation for modern-day veganism.

In November 1944, six non-dairy vegetarians including Donald Watson and Elsie Shrigley met together and discussed the topic on non-dairy vegetarians' lifestyles and diets. Despite strong opposition, these six members founded the new movement and became actively involved in this new project.

When the Vegan Society was formalized and registered as a charity organization in 1979, the Memorandum and Articles of Association of the society defined veganism as:

"...a philosophy and way of living which seeks to exclude – as far as possible and practicable – all forms of exploitation of, and cruelty to, animals for food, clothing or any other purpose; and by extension, promotes the development and use of animal-free alternatives for the benefit of humans, animals, and the environment. In dietary terms, it denotes the practice of dispensing with all products derived wholly or partly from animals."

This book deals only with the dietary aspect of veganism giving you amply sufficient reasons to shift your lifestyle to this healthy and noble one. While the benefits of turning vegan are discussed in another chapter, the kind of foods that you can include in your diet while keeping your energy levels and health not just unchanged but also improved than earlier is huge.

Here is a small list of foods that are known to be totally vegan:

- All kinds of grains and cereals
- All kinds of beans and legumes

- All fruits and vegetables

Other vegan foods include soy milk, vegan mayonnaise, vegan ice cream and cheese, vegan hot dogs, and more. Moreover, a lot of companies have come out with mock meats that give vegans a sense of eating meat. This book also has four chapters dedicated to making vegan foods, which includes easy-to-make recipes.

Chapter 1: Why Go Vegan?

Most people in the world want to do the following things by some means or the other:

- Lose weight
- Eat better
- Get fitter and healthier
- Do something for society and the world at large

The great news is that if you shift to a vegan diet, you can achieve all the above goals. And let me assure you, you will enjoy delicious, wholesome, and satiating meals as well.

No loss or reduction in energy levels – There is a misconception that changing to a vegan diet reduces your energy levels. There are numerous unworthy talks of vegans living only on water and a few greens and hence their energy levels have taken a huge dip. And on the other side of the spectrum, there are plenty of spurious rumors that talk of people going vegan is helping them do impossible things. These other-end-of-the-spectrum talks make out vegans to be people who can walk on water! Let me assure you that neither of the extremes is true or based on any scientific studies.

Health benefits are huge when you choose to go vegan. Of course, the initial learning curve is going to be steep and you would have to counter multiple challenges. However, once you have overcome these tough phases and complete the 30-day challenge, you are going feel to happier, lighter, and more fit. Moreover, there are multiple studies done by various organizations including the British Dietetic Association that has proven the excellent efficacies of getting fitter and healthier by following a vegan diet.

Here is the list of a few magic foods that can restore energy instantaneously:

Bananas – Already beautifully and naturally packaged by nature, this wonderful tropical fruit is normally the first you must reach out for when you feel tired or fatigued.

Walnuts – Another great pick-me-up tree nut, walnuts are rich in plant proteins, omega fatty acids, and vitamins giving you the almost-instant energy boost.

Green smoothies – Delicious smoothies made by tossing together strawberries, bananas, and orange juices are great and extremely healthy pick-me-ups to fight fatigue.

Coconut water – This is nature's energy drink and is amazingly refreshing and is filled with vitamins and potassium.

Kiwi – This low-fat delicious fruit is an instant energy enhancer triggered by the simple sugars present in it.

Why I chose to mention vegan energy boosters in the beginning itself is to help you overcome doubts regarding your ability to get on with your daily schedule if you choose to go vegan. Today there are many sportspeople who have shifted to this diet to keep fitter and sustain energy levels. So, if highly active people in the field of sports can take advantage of veganism, it should not be difficult for moderately active people like us to take this 30-day challenge and come out with flying colors.

Other great reasons to take the one-month challenge to go vegan are:

Lose weight and yet remain energized – Many of us would love to find a sensible way to lose excess weight and yet remain healthy and fit. Average vegans are known to weigh 20 pounds lesser than average meat-eaters. Despite this, vegan diets do not starve you and make you feel enervated like the usual run-of-the-meal fad diets do.

Keep diseases and health disorders away – The Academy of Nutrition and Dietetics have conducted multiple studies which show that taking the vegan route helps you steer clear of common disorders such as diabetes, hypertension or high blood pressure thereby preventing the onset of many modern-day diseases such as heart attacks, kidney failure, and others.

Vegan foods are yummy and delicious – If you thought going vegan means you would have to give up your favorite ice creams, hamburgers, and chicken sandwiches, then you are wrong. With demand for vegan products soaring, many companies are coming up with amazingly delicious vegan options that taste very much like the non-vegetarian stuff. You will not miss any of the meats and animal products at all. There are plenty of established brands that cater to veganism and deliver really tasty dairy and meat substitutes.

Vegan diets are full of highly nutritious and healthy food items including whole grains, beans and legumes, nuts, soy products, and fresh fruits and vegetables. Here are some of the health benefits that these fiber-rich and healthy food sources provide you with:

- **Minimal saturated fats** – Meats and dairy products contain plenty of saturated fats thereby increasing the risk of cardiovascular diseases. Vegan diets automatically reduce intake of saturated fats enhancing your health condition

- **Fiber** – A vegan diet is high in fiber content that is very conducive to healthy bowel movements.

- **Magnesium** – Dark, green leafy vegetables are a rich source of magnesium, a key element that aids the body in the absorption of calcium.

- **Potassium** – Similarly, potassium, an important mineral that balances acidity and water in our body and helps in the removal of toxins is found in plenty in plant-based foods.

- **Proteins** – Meat-eaters invariably end up with more proteins than is needed by the body. Vegan diets, which include nuts, beans, and legumes, have the right amount of proteins for us.

Vegan diets provide other critically essential nutrients such as Vitamins E and C, phytochemicals, antioxidants, and foliates. These help in keeping your immunity system healthy and robust and also prevent age-related diseases such as Alzheimer's and Parkinson's disease and keep your overall body organs functioning well.

Vegan diets have the power to prevent the following diseases that are very common in today's high-stressed unhealthy lifestyle:

- Cardiovascular diseases
- Reduced cholesterol due to the complete absence of meat and dairy products in your diet
- Age-related macular degeneration
- Reduced risk of breast cancer
- Reduced risk of contracting ailments like diabetes, hypertension, cataracts, colon and prostate cancer, arthritis, and osteoporosis

In addition to improved health and prevention of diseases, going vegan makes you stronger, more energetic, and more attractive. Here is how:

Lowered Body Mass Index – Cutting meat and dairy out of your diet naturally reduces Body Mass Index.

Weight loss – Weight loss is an unquestioned effect of a vegan diet.

Healthy skin – Consuming rich sources of Vitamins A and E from nuts and fruits and vegetables enhance the texture and health of your skin.

Reduced allergy symptoms – Plant-based foods do not trigger as many allergic reactions in humans as dairy and meat products do.

Less intake of mercury – A lot of shellfish and fish contain high levels of mercury, which we take in when we eat these foods. Switching to veganism does away with this toxin completely.

The above are only some of the great reasons that you must start off this 30-day vegan challenge. Instead of finding reasons not to do something good, focus on the above reasons which tell you why you should do it and dive straight in. Summon some extra willpower and after you complete this challenge you can rest assured that the willpower would come on its own when you see and feel the wondrous new VEGAN YOU.

Chapter 2: Understanding Vegan Diets

In the previous chapter, along with why should you go vegan, I had mentioned some basic foods that can deliver instant energy whenever you feel enervated. Just to reiterate, the foods listed are all completely vegan and yet are employed by all to get back energy levels when they feel sapped.

Considering the many misconceptions, doubts, and skepticism regarding energy levels and maintenance of good health by vegans, I thought it made sense to dedicate one chapter to help you overcome these misunderstandings which in turn will, I hope, will catapult your move to try out the 30-day vegan challenge.

There are many ex-vegans who complain of fogginess, depression, and other challenging mental and social circumstances when they chose to give up animal foods. Understanding the power and function of each nutrient is very helpful in managing those seemingly difficult days, especially during the initial adjustment phase of this diet.

Knowing how the various nutrients derived from animal and plant sources differ from each other, which vegan foods give you optimum results and how to keep feelings of depression at bay, due to short-term failures, are all critical elements in making a success of your 30-day vegan challenge. And when you come out successful in a small attempt, you will be emboldened to try for something bigger.

Carbohydrates for vegans – Cutting back on carbohydrates is not that difficult for anyone including for us vegans. It is essential for you to use low-carb food sources to maintain good health with a vegan diet.

Vegetables: There are many vegetables which are low-carb foods including onions, tomatoes, eggplant, cauliflower, broccoli, bell peppers, and more.

Fruits: Blueberries and strawberries are low-carb foods. However, depending on how much you need daily, other fruits can easily be included.

Fatty foods – Olives and avocados are high in good fats and low-carb too and hence excellent dietary inclusions for vegans.

Soy, nuts, and seeds: These are low in carbohydrates and high in fats and proteins. So, it is imperative to include soy, soy-based foods, nuts, and seeds into your daily diet.

Chia seeds: I deliberately included this one special item because most of the carbohydrates in chia seeds are in the form of fiber. Hence, most of the energy source from this food is got from fats and proteins. Do include chia seeds whenever you can.

Additionally, choose slow carbohydrate foods, that is, consume carb sources that have a low glycemic index. These foods prevent high fluctuations in your blood sugar levels and you will feel more satiated over a longer period as they release glucose slowly. For instance, choose breads that have been made from non-ground grains, use barley, quinoa, and oats in place of rice, use fresh beans and legumes instead of canned ones, use sweet potatoes instead of white potatoes.

Animal Protein Vs. Plant Protein – As our body does not accumulate protein, it is imperative that we take in proteins in our daily diet. Proteins are available both in plant-based and animal-based foods. The difference between the two sources is the profile of amino acid present. Amino acids are of different types (about 20 of them are very critical for us) and all of them are essential for carrying out multiple metabolic activities in our body.

Animal proteins invariably have a sufficiently wide range of amino acids in them whereas many plant proteins are not complete. For instance, many plant proteins are quite low in important amino acids such as tryptophan, methionine, isoleucine, and lysine. Legumes, on the other hand, are the best plant-based protein source that is comparable to meats. For this express reason, ensure you eat 3 servings of legumes daily in the form of peas, beans, peanuts, tofu etc. This will keep your energy levels optimum and considerably reduce your craving for meats.

Fats in vegan diets – Very low-fat foods are not great for vegan diets. In fact, a lot of recent studies have proved that very low-fat diets are not effective in the long-term. However, a free-for-all fatty diet is also an absolute no-no. It is important to include good-fat foods such as nuts and avocados to get the right quality and quantity of fat. Nutrition experts believe you should consume not more than 30 gm. of saturated fats every day.

Vitamins, Omega-3 fats, and other important nutrients – Animal protein foods contain higher levels and a wider range of other important nutrients such as Vitamins (B12 and D), DHA (Docosahexaenoic acid), which is an essential omega-3 fatty acid, zinc, and heme-iron. The four listed nutrients are found in abundance in meats such as pork, beef, dairy products, eggs, and fish, but are a little low in plant-based foods.

While this may seem a concern, let me assure you that there are ample solutions for this other than simply giving up a fantastically healthy lifestyle that has the power to change multiple things in a positive way (already discussed in the previous chapter). Omega-3 fatty acids are available in plenty in walnuts, flaxseed and flaxseed oil, and chia seeds. Vitamin B12 plant-based analogs include sourdough bread, fermented soy foods, shiitake mushrooms, and sea vegetables. Moreover, these trace nutritional elements like Vitamin B12, Vitamin D, iodine etc. can be easily taken as supplements.

Most plant-based foods are rich in folate (dark, green leafy veggies provide this nutrient in plenty), potassium, calcium (figs, nuts, almonds etc. are wonderfully rich in calcium), iron (lentils are a great source) Vitamin C, phytochemicals, and Vitamin A (carrots). So these nutrients are well covered in a vegan diet through the intake of ample amounts of differently colored fruits and vegetables.

Do not hesitate to use convenience foods – There are plenty of convenience products for vegans available in the market today. These include vegan ice creams, vegan meats, and vegan cheeses. When you are pressed for time and need convenience over laborious cooking processes, do not hesitate to use these options as they will go a long way in helping you stay committed to the vegan cause, especially in the early days when you are in the learning curve.

Chapter 3: Meal Plan and Outline Recipes for Block I

The next few chapters are dedicated to giving you meal plans along with some basic recipes and motivation for the start of your 30-day vegan challenge journey.

Day 1

"The secret of getting ahead is getting started."

- *Mark Twain*

Green smoothies for Breakfast

What to use:
- Mango juice (1/4 cup)
- Coconut Water (1/2 cup)
- Parsley (1/2 cup, fresh)
- Cilantro (1/2 cup, fresh)
- Avocado (1/2 – 1)
- Ice

What to do:
In a blender, mix mango juice and coconut water until the two are smoothly blended. Now add parsley, cilantro, avocado, and ice cubes and blend again to get a thick, super smooth smoothie. Adjust tartness and sweetness levels with sweetener choice to match your liking.

Lemon and Citrus Couscous with Fennel and Chickpeas for Lunch

What to use:
- Fennel (1 cup, trimmed)
- Chickpeas (2 cups, cooked)
- Coriander (1/4 cup)
- Couscous (3 cups)
- Lemon Juice (1 tbsp.)
- Kalamata Olives (1/3 cup)
- Orange Juice (1/3 cup)
- Citrus zest (1 ½ tbsp.)
- Olive oil (3 tbsp.)

What to do:

In a pan, cook the trimmed fennel until it reaches caramelization. To this, add cooked chickpeas, ground coriander, lemon juice, and kalamata olives and continue cooking over a medium flame until you have a nice veggie-filled sauce. To give the couscous a citrusy flavor, cook it in a mixture of orange juice and water along with some lemon and orange zest, a little olive oil, and salt. To serve this couscous meal, fluff up the couscous using a fork. Make a layer of the couscous plate and over it, spoon out the fennel and chickpeas mixture. You can now use the fennel frond for garnishing. Dig into your delicious vegan lunch.

***Tofu-Spinach Lasagna for Dinner* -**

What to Use:
- Lasagna noodles (24 oz.)
- Spinach (12 oz., frozen, chopped)
- Tofu (12 oz.)
- Sugar (1/4 tsp.)
- Soymilk (
- Lemon Juice (1 tbsp.)
- Garlic powder (1 tbsp.)
- Salt (1/2 tsp.)
- Basil (1 cup)
- Tomato Sauce (1 ½ cups)

What to do:
Cook the lasagna noodles as directed on the package, drain and keep aside. Squeeze the spinach to remove water as much as possible. In a blender, blitz together sugar, tofu, soymilk, lemon juice, garlic powder, salt, and basil until you get a smooth blend. Now, stir in the dried spinach. Take a baking dish and make a layer of tomato sauce at the bottom. Make a layer of the cooked lasagna noodles over this and over this a layer of the tofu mixture. Repeat the three layers again until all the materials are used up. The top layer should be that of the noodles and tomato sauce poured over it. In a preheated oven, bake this for about 25-30 minutes. Enjoy.

Day 2

"A wise man should consider that health is the greatest of human blessings, and learn how by his own thought to derive benefit from his illnesses."

- *Hippocrates*

Mango Smoothie for Breakfast -

What to use:
- Mango (frozen, 2 cups)
- Orange juice (1 ½ cups)
- Lime zest (½ tsp)
- Maple syrup (pure)

What to do:
Add 2 cups frozen mango, 1 ½ cup orange juice, ½ cup avocado, ½ tsp lime zest, pure maple syrup (to taste), and appropriate amount of water into a blender and blitz together everything until you get a lovely, thick, and creamy smoothie

Avocado and sauerkraut sandwiches for lunch -

What to Use:
- Dijon mustard (to taste)
- Bread (pumpernickel or rye)
- Vegan Thousand Island dressing (to taste)
- Sauerkraut (2 oz.)
- Avocado (1/2)

What to do:
Spread Dijon mustard on one slice of pumpernickel or rye bread and spread Thousand Island vegan dressing on the other slice. On an oiled (lightly) skillet, place the two slices (dry side down) and grill until golden brown. Pile on sauerkraut topping for one slice and avocado on the other slice. Continue to grill over medium heat for about 5 minutes. Remove from heat and join two halves and enjoy. Combine with cucumber and tomato salad for a complete vegan meal.

Scallion Pancakes for Dinner -

What to use:
- All-purpose flour (2 cups)
- Vegetable shortening (2 tsp.)
- Salt (1/2 tsp.)
- Green Onions (1/2 cup)
- Oil (1/4 cup)

What to do:
Make pancake dough with all-purpose flour, knead well and keep aside for some time. Then roll out the dough (1/8-inch thickness); spread a layer of vegetable shortening, and then sprinkle a layer of salt and then a layer of green onions. Gently roll this into a jelly-shaped roll and cut out fist-sized pieces. Again, with rolling pin, roll out each piece into 1/8-inch thick slices and cook on an oiled skillet until both sides for about 2 minutes each. Place the cooked pancakes on paper tissues to remove the excess oil and dig in. You could use soy sauce as a tartar dip.

Day 3

"If you're happy, if you're feeling good, then nothing else matters."

- *Robin Wright*

Chocolate Hemp Smoothie for Breakfast –

What to use:
- Almond Milk (2 cups)
- Pitted Dates (1/3 cup)
- Unsweetened cocoa powder (3 tbsp)
- Hemp seeds (3 tbsp)
- Banana (1, whole)
- Cinnamon (¼ tbsp)
- Ice

What to do:
In a blender add almond milk (2 cups), 1/3 cup pitted dates, 3 tbsp. unsweetened cocoa powder, 3 tbsp. hemp seeds (hulled), 1 banana (peeled and cut into slices/cubes), ¼ tsp cinnamon powder, and ice cubes. Blend it all together until the mixture reaches a thick, creamy, and smoothie-like (though this will be of a slightly thinner consistency) consistency. Pour into a glass and drink away.

Minestrone Soup and Crusty Bread for Lunch –

What to use:
- Olive oil (1 tbsp.)
- Onions (¾ cup, chopped)
- Zucchini (1/2 diced)
- Carrots (2, chopped)
- Beans (3 cups)
- Tomatoes (1 diced)
- Garlic (1 clove, minced)
- Celery (2 stalks, diced)
- Basil (1/4 cup)
- Pepper (1 tsp.)
- Salt (2/3 tsp.)
- Oregano (1 tsp.)

- Water (6 cups)
- Macaroni noodles (2 cups)

What to do:
In a saucepan, heat 1 tbsp. of olive oil (extra virgin) over medium heat. Sauté ¾ cup finely chopped onions, and add the following water, diced zucchini, carrots, beans, diced tomatoes, minced garlic, diced celery, dried basil, and pepper, oregano, and salt. Bring all this to a boil, and simmer for about 25-30 minutes until all ingredients are cooked. Now add ¼ cup macaroni and cook for another 10 minutes. Adjust spices to your taste and serve hot with some pumpernickel or rye bread (roasted on a skillet with a dash of oil).

Vegan sausages for dinner -

What to use:
- Beans (2 cups, personal choice for base)
- Olive oil (2 tsp.)
- Soy sauce (2 tbsp.)
- Garlic (1 clove, minced)
- Wheat gluten (1 tsp.)
- Yeast (1 tsp.)
- Fennel seeds (1/3 cup, crushed)
- Red pepper flakes (1/2 tbsp.)
- Pepper (2 tbsp.)
- Oregano (2 tbsp.)
- Salt (1 tbsp.)

What to do:
Get your steaming apparatus ready with water brought to a full boil. Cool and mash your chosen beans for a base nicely until no lumps are left. Add olive oil, soy sauce, finely minced garlic, wheat gluten, nutritional yeast, crushed fennel seeds, red pepper flakes, pepper, oregano, and salt and mix well until you get nice smooth dough-like consistency. Divide this dough into 4-6 portions and make each portion into a log shape (like the meat sausages). Place these on separate tin foils and roll the foil to look like a tootsie roll. Put these wrapped vegan sausages in the steamer and cook for about 40 minutes. Remove from heat and your vegan sausages are ready. Serve hot with a nice soy sauce dip or simply with ketchup.

Day 4

"Veganism is not a sacrifice. It is a joy."

- *Gary L. Francion*

Peanut Butter Banana Smoothie for Breakfast –

What to use:
- Bananas (2 whole, frozen)
- Dates (4 whole)
- Peanut butter (1 tsp)
- Chia seeds (1 tbsp)
- Water (¼ cup)

What to do:
In a blender, add 2 sliced frozen bananas, 4 small dates, 1 tbsp. peanut butter, 1 tbsp. chia seeds, and ¼ cup water. Blitz together until well blended and your smoothie is ready.

Asparagus, Potato, and Squash Frittata for Lunch -

Ingredients:

Squash (1, sliced)
Potatoes (2 sliced)
Garlic (1 clove, minced)
Italian Herbs (1 tsp.)
Onion (1/2 onion)
Salt (1 tsp.)
Pepper (2 tbsp.)
Asparagus (12 oz.)
Tofu (8 oz.)

Fry the squash and potatoes until golden brown. Next, add garlic, dried herbs, and onions and continue to sauté until the onions are soft. Add salt and pepper for seasoning. Now, put in the asparagus and stir over heat for a couple more minutes. Put this veggie mixture into cake tin. In a blender, blitz together tofu and other remaining ingredients (except the dried herbs) until smooth. Now add the herbs and mix well. Pour this tofu mixture onto the veggie layer. Smoothen out the tofu layer with a knife and bake for 30-40 minutes in a medium heat oven.

Tempeh Casserole for Dinner -

What to use:
- Tempeh (8 oz.)
- Onions (1 diced)
- Zucchini (1 sliced)
- Broccoli stock (2 cups)
- Brown rice (2 cups)
- Arrowroot starch (1 tbsp.)
- Balsamic vinegar (3 tbsp.)
- Herbs (2 tbsp.)
- Baking powder (1 tbsp.)
- Egg Substitute (1/4 cup)
- Vegan mayo (3 tsp.)
- Paprika (1/2 tsp.)
- Salt (1/4 tsp.)

What to do:
Mash the tempeh either in a food processor or with a potato masher. In a big bowl, mix this mashed tempeh with onions, zucchini, broccoli stock, brown rice, arrowroot starch, balsamic vinegar, herbs, baking powder, and egg substitute and place in a casserole dish. In a preheated oven at 350F, cook for about 20 minutes. For the sauce, combine vegan mayo, paprika, and salt. Serve hot.

Day 5

"As I improved my diet, I started to learn to love myself, probably for the first time ever."

- *Frank Ferrante*

Strawberry and Avocado Smoothie for Breakfast –

What to use:
- Banana (1/2 frozen)
- Strawberries (fresh, 2 cups)
- Spearmint (3 tbsp)
- Coconut water (1 ½ cups)
- Avocado (1/2)
- Date (pitted)
- Ice

What to do:
In a food processor, blend together ½ a frozen banana, 2 cups of fresh strawberries, 3 tbsp. of spearmint, 1 ½ cups of coconut water, ½ an avocado, 1 pitted date, and ice cubes. Your smoothie is ready to drink.

Adzuki Bean Burgers with Potato Wedges for Lunch -

What to use:
- Oats (1 package, prepackaged)
- Olive oil (1 tsp.)
- Celery (2 stalks, finely chopped)
- Onion (chopped)
- Garlic (1 clove)
- Carrots (2 chopped)
- Salt (1 tbsp.)
- Basil (3 tbsp.)
- Water (2 cups)
- Adzuki beans (1 cup)
- Parsley (2 tbsp.)
- Brown rice flour (1/4 cup)
- Bread (rye or pumpernickel)

What to do:
Boil the water in a saucepan and add a packet of oats. Simmer for about 2 minutes until the oats are cooked. Over a medium flame, heat 2 tbsp. of olive oil and put in celery, onions, garlic, and carrots and cook until tender. Add a little water, salt, and basil to this mixture and stir occasionally and cook for another 5 minutes.

In a food processor, blitz together the onion mixture, cooked oats, adzuki beans, and parsley. Stir in the brown rice flour until you get a dough-like consistency that can be molded into patties. Form 8-10 patties with this. Cook the patties on a skillet with a dash of oil. Place between toasted pumpernickel or rye bread and enjoy your meal.

Lentil and Barley Casserole for Dinner -

What to use:
- Oil (2 tbsp.)
- Onions (1 diced)
- Garlic (2 cloves, minced)
- Potatoes (3 diced)
- Swede (3 oz.)
- Carrots (3 chunked
- Rosemary (1 oz.)
- Bay leaves (1 oz.)
- Thyme (1 oz.)
- Tomato paste (1 cup)
- Water (2 cups)
- Pearl barley (2 oz.)
- Lentils (1/2 cup)
- Stock powder and cube (1 prepackaged)
- Mushrooms (2/3 cup)
- Pepper (1 tbsp.)

What to do:
In a large pan, heat oil and sauté the onions and garlic. Add potatoes, swede, and carrots (all cut into large chunks) and continue cooking until the veggies get tender. Put in rosemary, bay leaves, thyme, and tomato paste. Pour 5 cups of water and add pearl barley, lentils, stock powder, stock cube, and mushrooms. Add a little pepper for seasoning. Bring this mixture to a boil and then simmer over a low flame for about 45 minutes until a casserole consistency is achieved. Remove the bay leaves and then serve.

Day 6

"It's not a diet. It's not a phase. It's a permanent lifestyle."

- *Anonymous*

Cherry limeade Smoothie for Breakfast –

What to use:
- Peach (1 sliced)
- Cherries (frozen, 1 cup)
- Almond milk (¾ cup)
- Lime juice (1 lime, fresh squeezed)
- Ice

What to do:
In a blender, blend together 1 ripe peach (sliced), 1 cup frozen cherries, ¾ cup almond milk, juice of 1 lime, and some ice cubes. Your smoothie is ready.

Baked Potatoes and Coleslaw for Lunch -

What to use:
- Olive oil (1 tbsp.)
- Potatoes (6 whole)
- Vegan cream cheese (3 oz.)
- Vegan mayo (4 tsp.)
- Mustard (3 tsp.)
- Cabbage (2 cups, chopped)
- Carrots (1 cup, chopped)
- Onions (2/3 cup, chopped)

What to do:
Smear a little olive oil on the washed and dried potatoes and bake in a preheated oven for about 1 to 1 ½ hours until soft on the inside and crisp on the outside. For the coleslaw, combine cream cheese, vegan mayonnaise, and mustard until you get a smooth mixture. Add this to finely chopped cabbage, carrots, and onions, and mix well. Season as needed and refrigerate. When the potatoes are ready, cut in the middle and add the coleslaw and serve.

Noodles with vegetables and tofu for dinner -

What you need:
- Soy sauce (4 tsp.)
- Sweet chili sauce (2 tsp.)
- Mushroom sauce (2 tsp.)
- Noodles (24 oz.)
- olive oil (1 tsp.)
- Onions (1/2, chopped)
- Ginger (1 oz. grated)
- Garlic (1 clove, minced)
- Vegetables of choice
- Tofu (12 oz.)

What to do:
In a small bowl, mix together soy sauce, sweet chili sauce, and vegetarian mushroom sauce. In a large bowl, put a packet of noodles and cover completely with hot water. Close with a lid and set aside. Heat olive oil in a saucepan or wok and stir fry chopped onions for a minute. Now add ginger, garlic, and vegetables of your choice (such as carrots, zucchini, red Bell Pepper, and broccoli for example). Add some tofu too and fry further for 2-3 minutes. Use 5-spice powder for seasoning. Drain the liquid from the bowl of noodles. After removing all the water, add the noodles into the wok. Add the sauce mixture and mix everything well. Cook for another minute or two and serve hot.

Day 7

"When diet is wrong, medicine is of no use. When diet is correct, medicine is of no need."

- *Ayurvedic proverb*

Creamy Chocolate Shake for Breakfast –

What you need:
- Bananas (2, frozen)
- Strawberries (⅓ cup, frozen)
- Unsweetened cocoa powder (2-3 tbsp)
- Almond butter (2 tbsp)
- Flaxseed (1 tbsp)
- Non-dairy milk (1 ½-2 cups)
- Sweetener
- Ice

What to do:
In a blender, blitz together 2 ripe frozen bananas, 1/3 cup frozen strawberries, 2-3 tbsp. pure unsweetened cocoa powder, 2 tbsp. almond butter (salted), 1 tbsp. flaxseed meal, 1 ½ - 2 cups almond milk or soy milk or coconut milk, a dash of agave nectar or stevia, and some ice cubes. Your shake is ready

Vegetable and Pesto Sandwich for Lunch –

What you need:
- Zucchini (1 sliced)
- Eggplant (1 sliced)
- Bell Pepper (4 oz.)
- Onions (1 chopped)
- Pepper (2 tbsp.)
- Salt (1 tbsp.)
- Olive oil (1 tsp.)
- Pesto (dairy-free, to taste)
- Bread
- Lettuce (1 large leaf)
- Tomato (2 slices)

What to do:
Roast zucchini, eggplant, Bell Pepper, and onions along with seasoning of pepper, salt and olive oil in an oven until they turn soft and lightly brown. Spread dairy-free pesto on two bread slices and pile on the roasted veggies, tomato slices, and some lettuce leaves. Bring the slices together and your yummy veggie sandwich is ready.

Shepherd's pie for Dinner –

What you need:
- Potatoes (5)
- Salt (2 tsp.)
- Vegan margarine (3 oz.)
- Onions (1 chopped)
- Olive oil (1 tsp.)
- Zucchini (2 sliced)
- Mushrooms (1 cup)
- Carrots (3 chopped)
- Tomato paste (2 cups)
- Canned tomatoes (1 can)
- Stock cube (1)
- Herbs
- Vegan Mince
- Gravy powder (1 package)

What to do:
Boil, peel and mash some potatoes with a little salt and some vegan margarine. Sauté onions with some olive oil in a saucepan until tender and to this add chopped zucchini, mushrooms, and carrots. After the veggies have softened add tomato paste, canned tomatoes, stock cube, herbs and casserole mince and stir well. Make thick gravy with gravy powder and some water and pour into this veggie mix. Cool for about 25-30 minutes. In a baking tray, pour this veggie mixture and layer the mashed potato mix on top. Bake this dish for around 25-30 minutes or until the top is nicely browned.

Day 8

"The future depends on what we do in the present."

- *Gandhi*

5-ingredient healthy delicious smoothie for breakfast –

What you need:
- Mixed berries (1 cup, frozen)
- Spinach (2 handfuls, fresh)
- Mixed fruit juice (2-3 cups)
- Banana (1 frozen)
- Flaxseed (1/4 cup)

What to do:
In a blender, blitz together frozen berry mix, spinach, flaxseed, mixed fruit juice, and a frozen banana and your delicious breakfast smoothie is ready.

Peking Mock "duck" pancakes for lunch –

What you need:
- Vegan "duck" (12 oz.)
- Duck sauce (5 tsp.)
- Vegan pancake batter (1 prepackaged)
- Onions (1 shredded)
- Cucumber (1 thinly sliced)

What to do:
Thaw the mock duck and put into a baking dish. Slather it with Peking duck sauce and bake for about 30 minutes at 200C. Shred the baked mock duck. Use ready made vegan pancake batter and cook the pancakes as directed. To serve, take a pancake, layer with Peking duck sauce, add shredded onions, cucumbers, and the mock duck and roll it gently. Your savory pancake is ready to enjoy.

Eggplant and Tomato Pasta for Dinner –

What to use:
- Olive Oil (2 tsp.)
- Onions (1 sliced)

- Garlic (2 cloves, minced)
- Eggplant (1 chopped)
- Balsamic vinegar (2 tsp.)
- Tomatoes (1 canned)
- Tomato Paste (1 can)
- Herbs
- Sun-dried tomatoes (1 cup)
- Chili Flakes (1 ½ tsp.)
- Sugar (1 tsp.)
- Water (2 cups)

What to do:

In a large pan, add olive oil and sauté onions and minced garlic cloves. Add chopped eggplant and balsamic vinegar and cook until the veggies are soft and tender. Now add canned tomatoes, tomato paste, dried herbs, sun-dried tomatoes, chili flakes (if you like, add spice), sugar and some water. Bring this mixture to a full boil and cook it down for about half an hour. Cook the pasta separately and drain the excess water. Add the cooked pasta to the cooked veggie mixture and mix well. Add basil for improved flavor, to taste.

You are halfway done!

Congratulations on making it to the halfway point of the journey. Many try and give up long before even getting to this point, so you are to be congratulated on this. You have shown that you are serious about getting better every day. I am also serious about improving my life, and helping others get better along the way. To do this I need your feedback. Click on the link below and take a moment to let me know how this book has helped you. If you feel there is something missing or something you would like to see differently, I would love to know about it. I want to ensure that as you and I improve, this book continues to improve as well. Thank you for taking the time to ensure that we are all getting the most from each other.

Chapter 4: Meal Plan and Outline Recipes for Block II

Day 9

"Vegan food is soul food in its truest form. Soul food means to feed the soul. And to me, your soul is your intent. If your intent is pure, you are pure."

- *Erykah Bad*

Blueberry maple and protein shake for breakfast –

What to use:
- Low-fat yogurt (3 cups)
- Vanilla protein powder (1 scoop)
- Blueberries (frozen, ½ cup)
- Maple extract (2 tsp.)
- Flaxseed (1/3 cup)
- Ice

What to do:
In a blender, mix low-fat yogurt, 1 scoop of vanilla protein powder, ½ cup blueberries (frozen), maple extract (to taste), flaxseed meal, and some ice cubes. Your delicious and nutritious breakfast shake is ready

Veggie fritters for lunch –

What to use:
- All-purpose flour (2 cups)
- Soy milk (2/3 cup)
- Choice of vegetables (1/2 cup)
- Salt (1 tbsp.)
- Pepper (1 tbsp.)
- Oil (1 tsp.)

What to do:
Mix all-purpose flour and soy milk to form batter for the fritters. Stir in sliced vegetables of your choice (zucchini, carrots, potatoes, broccoli florets, onions) and

season with salt and pepper. Heat a little oil in a large skillet and spoon out a little of this mixture at a time giving it a round flat shape. Flip over and cook the other side after one side is cooked. Remove from heat, drain excess oil on tissue paper and serve hot.

Saucy tofu skewers for dinner – Cut out tofu and all your favorite veggies in roughly the same size squares. Place them on a bamboo or metal skewer. Cover with any of your favorite vegan sauces and leave to marinate for some time Barbecue or grill on a skillet until cooked. Serve with extra sauce.

Day 10

"Nothing will benefit human health and increase the chances for survival of life on Earth as much as the evolution to a vegetarian diet."
— Albert Einstein

Kale-based smoothie for breakfast –

What to use:
- Banana (1 whole)
- Mixed berries (frozen, ½ cup)
- Hemp seeds (1 tbsp)
- Kale (2 cups)
- Pomegranate juice (⅔ cup)
- Water

What to do:
In a food blender, blitz together 1 banana (medium ripe), ½ cup mixed berries (frozen), 1 tbsp. hulled hemp seeds, 2 cups kale leaves (fresh or frozen), 2/3 cup pomegranate juice, and some water (depending on the consistency you like; less water if you want a thick smoothie and more water if you want a thin smoothie).

Parsnip and Tempeh Rolls for lunch –

What to use:
- Garlic (1 clove, minced)
- Onions (1 diced)
- Oil (2 tsp.)
- Cumin (1 tbsp.)
- Sage (1 ½ oz.)
- Marjoram (2 oz.)
- Thyme (1 oz.)
- Salt (1 tbsp.)
- Pepper (1 tbsp.)
- Parsnip (2 chopped)
- Tempeh (6 oz.)
- Worcestershire sauce (anchovy free)

- Water
- Soy sauce (2 tsp.)
- Phyllo pastry sheets

What to do:
Fry garlic and onions in a little oil until soft and add spices including cumin powder, dried sage, marjoram, thyme, salt and pepper and cook until the aromas are released. Add grated parsnip and tempeh to this mixture until soft. Add anchovy-free Worcestershire sauce, water, and soy sauce and cook (stirring continuously) for 4-5 minutes more until the parsnips are fully cooked. Season with salt and pepper and keep aside.

Cut pastry sheets such that you can make rectangle rolls. Spread the tempeh and parsnip filling over the pastry, then fold over the pastry sheet and press the meeting ends together to seal well. Then cut these filled portions into bite-sized pieces. Bake them in a preheated oven at 180C for about 15 minutes or until they are golden brown.

Chili non-carne for dinner -

What to use:
- Onions (1 chopped)
- Garlic (2 cloves, minced)
- Zucchini (1 sliced)
- Carrots (2 sliced)
- Mushrooms (1 cup)
- Bell Pepper (1 chopped)
- Cumin (2 tbsp.)
- Coriander (1 tbsp.)
- Fennel seeds (2 tsp.)
- Chili flakes (1 tsp.)
- Peppercorns (1 tbsp.)
- Paprika (1 tbsp.)
- Canned Tomatoes (1 can)
- Tomato Paste (1 can)
- Kidney beans (3 cups)
- Stock cube

What to do:
In a big saucepan, fry onions and garlic until soft. Add zucchini, carrots,

mushrooms, and Bell Pepper and fry some more until veggies are all tender. Add a spice mixture consisting of cumin powder, coriander powder, fennel seeds, chili flakes, peppercorns, paprika, and salt. Cook for some more time until the spices release aroma. To this add canned tomatoes, tomato paste, kidney beans (canned) and stock cube. Simmer for about half an hour and your non-carne is ready. Serve with rice, baked potatoes, enchiladas, or tacos.

Day 11

"Raw food is the best way to have the cleanest energy. We take so much care about what kind of fuel we put in our car, what kind of oil. We care about that sometimes more than the fuel that we're looking at putting in our bodies. It's cleaner burning fuel."
- *Woody Harrelson*

Mango Green Smoothie for breakfast–

What to use:
- Mango (frozen, 1 ½ cups)
- Strawberries (frozen, 1 cup)
- Spinach (1 cup, fresh)
- Almond milk (1 cup)
- Sweetener

What to do:
In a blender, blitz together 1 ½ cups of frozen mango, 1 cup frozen strawberries, 1 cup spinach (fresh), 1 cup almond milk, and a vegan sweetener like stevia or agave. Your mango green smoothie is ready.

Spicy Couscous for lunch –

What to use:
- Olive oil (2 tsp.)
- Onions (1/2 chopped)
- Garlic (1 clove, minced)
- Bell Pepper (1 chopped)
- Zucchini (1 sliced)
- Cumin (1 tsp.)
- Coriander (1 tsp.)
- Pepper (1 tbsp.)
- Fennel (1 tbsp.)
- Chili flakes (1 tbsp.)
- Salt (1 tbsp.)
- Couscous (2 cups)
- Water (boiling)
- Chickpeas (cooked)

- Stock powder (1 package)
- Sun-dried tomatoes (2/3 cup)

What to do:
In a large pan, heat some olive oil and sauté onions and garlic until translucent. Add Bell Pepper and zucchini and cook until soft. Add spice mixture consisting of cumin, coriander, black pepper, fennel, chili flakes, and salt. Fry for another minute until the aromas of the spices are released. Stir in some couscous and add boiling water and some stock powder into this veggie mixture. Now add some sun-dried tomatoes and cooked chickpeas to this and mix thoroughly. Cover the pan with a lid and put off the heat and let it be for about 5 minutes. Once the couscous has absorbed all the stock, sprinkle some freshly chopped coriander and your lunch is ready.

Thai Red Curry for Dinner –

What to use:
- Onions (1 chopped)
- Red curry paste (2 tsp.)
- Coconut milk (1 cup)
- Vegetable stock (2 cups)
- Tofu (8 oz.)
- Mushrooms (1 cup)
- Sugar (2 tsp.)
- Soy sauce (1 tsp.)
- Bell Pepper (1 chopped)
- Bamboo shoots (1/3 cup)
- Chili (2 tsp.)
- Sugar snap peas (2 cups)

What to do:
Fry onions in a little bit of oil until tender. To this add 2 tbsp. of red curry paste (ensure that the paste has no shrimp paste in it). Stir for a while and then slowly add coconut milk in small amounts stirring continuously. Now add vegetable stock. Bring this mixture to a boil and then reduce the heat to allow it to simmer.

Add tofu, mushroom, sugar, soy sauce, and Bell Pepper to this mixture and continue to simmer for 10 more minutes. Now add bamboo shoots, chili, and sugar snap peas and cook for another 5 minutes. Serve with steamed rice.

Day 12

"Strive for progress, not perfection."

- *Unknown*

Mango-Strawberry with lime smoothie for breakfast –

What to use:
- Mangoes (2, cubed)
- Strawberries (frozen, ½ cup)
- Lime juice (half lime)
- Ice

What to do:
In a blender, blitz together 2 mangoes (cubed), ½ a cup frozen strawberries, lime juice (from half a lime), and ice cubes. Your lime mango-strawberry smoothie is ready.

Asparagus and Pine Nut Tart for lunch –

What to use:
- Pastry sheet
- Mustard (1/2 tsp.)
- Asparagus (5 pieces)
- Vegan cream cheese (1 tsp.)
- Non-dairy milk (1 tbsp)
- Vegan cheese (to taste)
- Pine nuts (1/3 cup)

What to do:
Cut a sheet of pastry into two such as that you have 2 equal rectangles. At ½ cm from the edge, gently score the 4 sides of the pastry. Spread some mustard on the pastry sheet and place 5 asparagus sticks on each of the two rectangles (within the scored line). Bake until the pastry starts to rise. Mix together vegan cream cheese and 1 tbsp. non-dairy milk. Pour this mixture over the pastry and sprinkle some vegan cheese over. Put the pastry in the oven again and bake for about 10 minutes until golden brown. Remove from the oven and sprinkle roasted pine nuts over the tarts. Enjoy.

Tacos and Guacamole for dinner –

What to use:
- Prepared chili non-carne
- Taco size tortillas
- Salad leaf mixture
- Guacamole
- Salsa

What to do:
First, make the chili non-carne (recipe described in Day 10 dinner meal). First, heat the soft taco shells in a skillet and then fill them with salad leaves, guacamole, salsa, and chili non-carne. Your simple yet delicious taco meal is ready.

Day 13

"Strength does not come from physical capacity. It comes from an indomitable will."
- *Mahatma Gandhi*

Jelly Dates and Peanut butter smoothie for breakfast –

What to use:
- Medjool dates (4)
- Peanut butter (1 tbsp)
- Banana (1 frozen)
- Almond milk (¾ cup)
- Blueberries (frozen, 1/3 cup)
- Flaxseed (1 tbsp)

What to do:
In a blender, blitz together 4 Medjool dates, 1 tbsp. peanut butter, 1 frozen banana, ¾ cup almond milk, 1/3 cup frozen blueberries, and 1 tbsp. flaxseed meal. Blend until desired smooth consistency. Your jelly dates and peanut butter smoothie is ready for enjoyment.

Pumpkin soup for lunch –

What to use:
- Oil
- Onions (1 chopped)
- Pumpkin squash (2 chunked)
- Water (boiling)
- Noodle soup packet (1 packaged)
- Salt (1 tsp.)
- Pepper (1 tsp.)

What to do:
In a large pan, heat up some oil and sauté onions and pumpkin squash chunks until they start to brown. Pour boiling water until the veggies are completely covered and then stir in 1 packet of noodle soup. Simmer the pan contents until the pumpkin squash is cooked through. Blend this entire mixture and season with salt and pepper. Serve with some crusty bread.

Marinated Tempeh Steak with Veggies for dinner –

What to use:
- Tempeh (4 blocks)
- Garlic (1 clove, minced)
- Soy sauce (2 tsp.)
- Oil (2 tsp.)
- Pine nuts (1/3 cup)
- Asparagus (6 oz.)
- Baby potatoes (2 cups)
- Vegan margarine
- Parsley (1/3 cup)

What to do:
Slice the tempeh block into two thinner pieces and then cut these again so that you get 4 blocks of tempeh altogether. Marinate these tempeh blocks with garlic-infused soy sauce for as long as you can. Drizzle some oil in a skillet and fry the marinated tempeh until both the sides are brown.

For the veggies, roast pine nuts and steam the asparagus spears. Steam baby potatoes until they are soft. Toss the boiled potatoes with some vegan margarine in a hot skillet and chopped parsley. Plate the tempeh and arrange all the veggies on the side.

Day 14

"Energy and persistence conquer all things."
- *Benjamin Franklin*

Berry, Banana, and Sesame Smoothie for breakfast –

What to use:
- Banana (1 whole)
- Wheat germ (4 tbsp.)
- Sesame seeds (4 tbsp)
- Strawberries (fresh, 5)
- Yogurt (berry flavored, 2 tbsp)

What to do:
Put 1 small banana, 1 tbsp. wheat germ, 4 tbsp. of sesame seeds, 5 strawberries, and 2 tbsp. of berry-flavored yogurt and blend until smooth. Pour into a glass and have a wholesome vegan breakfast.

Tempeh strips with salad wraps for lunch –

What to use:
- Tempeh (12 oz.)
- Garlic (2 cloves, minced)
- Canola oil (1 tbsp.)
- Sesame oil (1 tsp.)
- Vegan margarine (1 tsp.)
- Beetroot dip (3 tsp.)
- Wrap
- Fresh veggies of choice

What to do:
Marinate tempeh with a garlic infused mixture of canola and sesame oils. After marination cut into strips and cook in a hot skillet until both sides are brown. Spread vegan margarine and beetroot dip on the ready-to-eat wraps and fill the wraps with tempeh strips and your veggies (cut into strips).

Lentil Dahl for dinner –

What to use:
- Garlic (1 clove, minced)
- Onion (1 chopped)
- Vegetable oil (2 tsp.)
- Cumin (1 tbsp.)
- Ginger (2 tbsp. grated)
- Turmeric (1 tbsp.)
- Garam masala (1 tbsp.)
- Lentils (2 cups)
- Cardamom pods
- Stock powder
- Cinnamon (1 tbsp.)
- Bay leaves

What to do:
In a saucepan, fry garlic and onions in a little bit of vegetable oil until onions are translucent. Add cumin, ginger, turmeric powder, and garam masala powder and continue to fry until the aromas of the spices are released. Now add some water, lentils, cardamom pods, stock powder, cinnamon powder, and bay leaves. Cook, while stirring occasionally, for about 25 minutes until the mixture is fully cooked. Serve hot with rice or your favorite crusty bread.

Day 15

"Ability is what you're capable of doing. Motivation determines what you do. Attitude determines how well you do it."
- *Lou Holtz*

Cheesecake strawberry smoothie for breakfast –

What to use:
- Strawberries (1 cup)
- Oil
- Vegan Cottage cheese (1 cup)
- Chia seeds (1/3 cup)
- Sweetener
- Ice

What to do:
First, roast the strawberries with any vegetable oil and bake for about 20 minutes until the juices of the berries are released. Now, in a blender, blitz together cottage cheese, roasted strawberries, chia seeds, a sweetener like an agave or stevia, and ice cubes. Pour the smoothie into a glass and enjoy your breakfast.

Vegetable burger and raw salad for lunch –

What to use:

- Prepared vegetable or bean burger patty
- Fresh vegetables and leafy greens
- Lime juice (to taste)
- Agave (to taste)

What to do:
Heat up a ready-to-eat vegetable or red lentil burger until brown on both sides. Chop up some favorite vegetables like cucumber, tomatoes, cabbage, and baby spinach and make a salad with a simple lime juice and agave dressing. Enjoy your lunch of vegetable burger and salad.

Roast with cooked Vegetables for dinner –

What to use:

- Potatoes (2 diced)
- Butternut squash (1 diced)
- Zucchini (2 chopped)
- Carrots (3 chopped)
- Corn
- Onions (1 chopped)
- Garlic (2 cloves minced)
- Rosemary
- Bell Pepper (3 chopped)
- Vegan roast

What to do:
In a greased baking pan, place potatoes, butternut squash, zucchini, carrots, corn, onions, and garlic and sprinkle some rosemary over. Cover the pan with aluminum foil and bake at 180C in a preheated oven for about 30 minutes. Remove the vegan roast from the packet and rub with olive oil, rosemary, and mint. Once the veggies have cooked for 30 minutes, place the roast in the middle, add some Bell Pepper and bake for another half hour. Serve with garlic bread and a mushroom gravy.

Day 16

"Motivation is what gets you started. Habit is what keeps you going."
- *Jim Ryan*

Raspberry-banana smoothie for breakfast –

What to use:
- *Banana (1 frozen)*
- Raspberries (frozen, 1 ¼ cup)
- Orange juice (¾ cup)
- Pomegranate juice (½ cup)
- Almond milk (unsweetened, ¾ cup)

What to do:
In a food processor, blend together 1 large, ripe banana (frozen), 1 ¼ cup raspberry (frozen), ¾ cup orange juice, ½ cup pomegranate juice, and ¾ cup unsweetened almond milk. Your raspberry-banana smoothie is ready.

Sweet corn and cauliflower soup for lunch –

What to use:
- Cauliflower head (1/2)
- Corn on cob (2)
- Potato (1 large, diced)
- Leek (1)
- Vegetable stock (1 cup)
- Salt (1 tbsp.)
- Pepper (1 tbsp.(
- Water (2 cups)

What to do:
In a big saucepan, put a ½ head of cauliflower (cut into florets), kernels from 2 corn cobs, 1 large potato (diced), 1 small leek, 1 cup of vegetable stock, salt, and pepper and one liter of water. Bring this mixture to a boil and then simmer on a low flame for about 15-20 minutes until veggies are cooked through. Cool and then blend in a food processor. Serve hot with crusty bread.

Spaghetti Bolognese for dinner –

What to use:
- Onions (1/2 chopped)
- Garlic (1 clove minced)
- Mushrooms (1 cup)
- Zucchini (1 sliced)
- Carrots (2 chopped)
- Tomatoes (canned)
- Worcestershire sauce (2 tsp. anchovy free)
- Tomato paste (1 can)
- Stock cube
- Herbs
- Spaghetti (1 box)

What to do:
In a large saucepan, fry onions and garlic with some oil until soft. Now add mushrooms, zucchini, and carrots, stir gently and cook for 2-3 minutes. Now add canned tomatoes, anchovy-free Worcestershire sauce, tomato paste, stock cube, and herbs and mix well. Season the mixture with salt and pepper. Simmer for about 20 minutes. Cook and drain spaghetti as directed on the packet and serve with the sauce.

Chapter 5: Meal Plan and Recipes for Block III

"Clear your mind of can't."
- *Samuel Johnson*

Day 17

Peach Oat Smoothie for breakfast –

What to use:
- Peaches (2 cubed)
- Chia seeds (1 tbsp)
- Banana (1/2)
- Uncooked oats (¼ cup)
- Almond milk (unsweetened, ½ cup)
- Orange juice ¼ cup
- Agave (optional)

What to do:
In a blender, blitz together 2 ripe peaches (cut into cubes), 1 tbsp. chia seeds, ½ frozen banana, ¼ cup uncooked oats, ½ cup almond milk (unsweetened), ¼ orange juice, and agave (if you want). Your peach oat smoothie is done.

Stir Fry Veggies and Tempeh with rice for lunch –

What to use:
- Oil (1 tsp.)
- Stir fry vegetables (2 cups)
- Choice of spices
- Tempeh (1 ½ cups)
- Soy sauce (2 tsp.)
- Sweet chili sauce (1 tsp.)

What to do:
Place some oil in a large pan and stir fry vegetables of your choice such as broccoli florets, carrots, zucchini, mushrooms, onions, and whatever else you like to stir fry. Add spices like curry powder, cumin powder, and coriander powder and continue to stir fry until all veggies are tender. Add some tempeh (cut into squares) and then add a mixture of soy sauce and sweet chili sauce. Toss everything together and

serve on a plate of steamed hot rice.

Soy strips Rougaille with a watercress salad for dinner –

What to use:
- Olive Oil (2 tsp.)
- Onions (1 chopped)
- Garlic (1 clove minced)
- Thyme
- Ginger (1 oz.)
- Tomato paste (1 can)
- Tomatoes (1 diced)
- Chili (1 tsp.)
- Soy strips (1 package)
- Watercress (3 oz.)
- Carrots (2 chopped)
- Bell Pepper (2 chopped)
- Orange juice (1/3 cup)
- Salt (1 tbsp.)
- Pepper (1 tbsp.

What to do:
In a large pan, heat some oil and sauté onions, garlic, thyme, and some ginger. Add tomato paste, tomatoes, and some chili and let it simmer for 2 minutes. In another pan, fry marinated soy strips in olive oil until brown. To the simmering sauce add the fried soy strips with some water and bring to a boil. Then reduce the heat and allow it to simmer for about 10 minutes or until the sauce thickens. For the watercress salad, toss together chopped watercress, carrots, and Bell Pepper along with vinaigrette of orange juice, salt, and pepper. Place the salad on a plate and over this place the sauce-filled soy strips. Enjoy your dinner

Day 18

"Our greatest weakness lies in giving up. The most certain way to succeed is always to try just one more time."

- *Thomas Edison*

Banana bread smoothie for breakfast –

What to use:
- Banana (1 frozen)
- Quinoa (cooked, ½ cup)
- Walnuts (1 tbsp)
- Flaxseed (2 tbsp)
- Date (1)
- Cinnamon (¾ tsp)
- Ice

What to do:
Place 1 frozen banana, ½ cup quinoa (cooked), 1 tbsp. walnuts. 2 tbsp. flaxseed, 1 Medjool date, ¾ tsp cinnamon powder, and some ice cubes. Blitz together, pour into your glass and enjoy your smoothie.

Crispy Mock Chicken with Potato Mash for lunch –

What to use:
- Mock chicken breast (1 prepackaged)
- Oil
- Mashed Potatoes (4 potatoes, mashed)

What to do:
Cut "mock" chicken into chunks or strips and put them into a Ziploc pouch along with seasoning and breadcrumbs for about 30 minutes. Heat some oil in a pan, and fry this in batches until golden brown. Serve on a plate of hot mashed potatoes.

Avocado on Toast for dinner –

What to use:
- Bread

- Vegan margarine
- Avocados (2 whole)
- Fresh veggies (optional)

What to do:
Take a slice of your favorite bread and toast with some vegan margarine until golden brown. Pile mashed avocados over this and enjoy a healthy and extremely easy-to-make vegan meal. You could add some sprouts and raw veggies for some crunch and extra energy.

Day 19

"Setting goals is the first step in turning the invisible into the visible."

- *Tony Robbins*

Green Apple and Cucumber Smoothie for breakfast –

What to use:
- Green apple (1 chopped)
- Walnuts (1 tbsp)
- Cucumber (1/2)
- Avocado (1/4)
- Agave (optional)
- Ice

What to do:
In a blender, blitz together chopped green apple, 1 tbsp. walnuts, ½ a cucumber, ¼ of an avocado (chopped), some agave (if you want), and ice cubes. Your delicious green apple and cucumber smoothie is ready.

Enchiladas and Guacamole for lunch –

What to use:
- Prepared chili non-carne
- Tortillas (1 package)
- Salsa (4 oz.)
- Guacamole (6 oz.)

What to do:
First, make some chili non-carne as described in an earlier meal plan day (specifically Day 10's dinner recipe). Get yourself some ready made tortillas and salsa, or create your own salsa by running onions, tomatoes, garlic, jalapenos or chili of choice, lime juice and fresh cilantro through a food processor. On a tortilla, spread some chili non-carne, and fold it over. Bake until the tortillas are slightly brown. Remove from the oven and place some salsa on top. Serve hot with some fresh guacamole.

Bombay potatoes with pita bread for dinner –

What to use:
- Bombay potato packet (1 prepackaged)
- Pita bread
- Vegan sour cream (3 oz.)
- Coriander (1 oz.)

What to do:
Heat the packet of Bombay potatoes and cook as directed. Warm the pita bread and spread the potatoes in a layer on the top. Garnish the pita with some vegan sour cream and some fresh coriander. Dig right in.

Day 20

"I attribute my success to this: I never gave or took any excuse."

- *Florence Nightengale*

***Strawberries smoothie for breakfast* –**

What to use:
- Strawberries (frozen, 1 cup)
- Chia seeds (1/3 cup)
- Flaxseed (1/3 cup)
- Oats (2/3 cup)
- Apple cider vinegar (2 tsp.)
- Vanilla extract (2 tbsp.)
- Ice

What to do:
Place 1 cup frozen strawberries, some chia seeds, some flaxseed, raw oats, apple cider vinegar, vanilla extract, and some ice cubes. Blitz all together with a blender and your smoothie is ready.

***Roasted vegetable lasagna for lunch* –**

What to use:
- Eggplant (1 chopped)
- Bell Pepper (2 chopped)
- Zucchini (1 chopped)
- Onions (1 chopped)
- Olive oil (2 tsp.)
- Salt (1 tbsp.)
- Pepper (1 tbsp.)
- Pesto
- Tomatoes (2 diced)
- Tomato paste (1 can)
- Vegan margarine
- Flour (2/3 cup)
- Vegan cream cheese (1/3 cup)
- Lasagna noodles (1 package)

What to do:
In a baking dish, put together chopped eggplant, Bell Pepper, zucchini, and onions. Drizzle some olive oil and season vegetable mixture with salt and pepper. Toss it all together and bake in a medium heated oven until tender. Once this is cooled, add pesto, chopped tomatoes, and tomato paste and mix thoroughly.

Make a white sauce with vegan margarine, flour, and vegan cream cheese. Now, take a baking dish, make a vegetable layer at the bottom; next place a lasagna sheet, and then pour the white sauce over. Repeat this layering process until the ingredients are all used up. Bake for about 30-40 minutes until the top is lightly brown. Enjoy your vegan lasagna hot.

One-pot Black Bean Chili for dinner-

What to use:
- Carrots (2 chopped)
- Peppers (2 chopped)
- Onion (1 chopped)
- Diced tomatoes (1 diced)
- Cumin (1 tsp.)
- Garlic (1 clove, minced)
- Paprika (1 tsp.)
- Chili powder (1 tsp.)
- Black beans (1 ½ cups)
- Corn (1 cup, frozen)
- Vegan cheese (optional)

What to do:
In a large pan sauté carrots, peppers, and onion until tender. After sautéed add diced tomatoes and seasonings such as cumin, garlic, paprika and chili powder. Mix these ingredients well and add in black beans and corn kernels. Let simmer a while before eating for spices to fully blend flavors. Distribute to a bowl and top with vegan cheese, served most deliciously with crusty bread or a baked potato.

Day 21

"Outstanding people have one thing in common: An absolute sense of mission."

- *Zig Ziglar*

Green Smoothie for breakfast –

What to use:
- Cucumber (1)
- Spinach (3 cups, raw)
- Melon (2 cups)
- Green tea (1 cup)
- Lemon juice (1 tsp.)
- Agave (optional)
- Ice

What to do:
Blend together 1 cucumber (diced), 3 cups of spinach (raw), 2 cups melon (cubed), some brewed green tea, a little lemon juice (for tartness), some agave (if you want), and some ice cubes. Once nicely blended pour into a glass and enjoy your breakfast.

Stir-fry vegetables with marinated soy strips for lunch –

What to use:
- Oil
- Favorite vegetables
- Soy strips (marinated)
- Seasonings and sauce of choice

What to do:
In a large pan, with a little oil, stir-fry all your favorite veggies along with some marinated soy strips. Add spices and sauces of your choice. Serve on a plate of hot steamed rice.

Vegan hot dogs for dinner –

What to use:
- Vegan hot dogs (2)

- Vegan margarine
- Bun (2)
- Mustard (to taste)
- Cucumber (1/2 thinly sliced)
- Tomato (1/2 thinly sliced)
- Lettuce (a few leaves)

What to do:
Cook the ready made vegan hot dogs by boiling, steaming, or frying. Spread vegan margarine on one side of the bun (cut in half), smear mustard on the other half, place the hot dogs in the middle and pile on cucumbers and tomato slices and some lettuce leaves. Bring the two halves of the bun together and your dinner is ready.

Day 22

"Nothing is impossible; the word itself says 'I'm possible!'"

- *Audrey Hepburn*

Mint and chocolate chip smoothie for breakfast –

What to use:
- Peppermint tea (1 cup)
- Almond milk (1 cup, unsweetened)
- Banana (1 frozen)
- Spinach (2 cups, fresh)
- Hemp seeds (1 tsp)
- Chocolate chips (1/3 cup)
- Ice

What to do:
Place a peppermint tea in boiling water and get a nicely concentrated cup of peppermint tea ready. In a blender, put together 1 cup unsweetened almond milk, 1 frozen banana, 2 cups of spinach, 1 tsp of hemp seeds, 2 tbsp. of chocolate chips, and ice cubes. Blitz everything and pour into a glass. Put some more chocolate chips on top and your breakfast is ready.

Thai noodles for lunch –

What to use:
- Vermicelli noodles (1 package)
- Olive oil
- Chopped stir fry vegetables of choice (2 cups)
- Soy sauce (1 tsp.)
- Sesame oil (1 tsp.)

What to do:
Cook vermicelli noodles as directed on the packet. Drain and keep aside. Heat some olive oil in a large pan and add chopped veggies like celery, bok choy, spring onions, mushrooms, peanuts, chili, ginger, and garlic. Cook until the vegetables are tender. Make a mixture of light soy sauce and sesame oil. Once the vegetables are nicely tender, stir in the noodles and add the sauce mixture. Mix well. Remove

from heat and serve hot.

Sandwich with soy strips for dinner –

What to use:
- Bread
- Marinated soy strips (1 package)
- Raw vegetables of choice (sliced)
- Vegan margarine
- Dijon mustard (to taste)

What to do:
Make a yummy sandwich with your favorite bread slices and marinated soy strips. Add some raw vegetables for some crunch. You can use vegan margarine and Dijon mustard as sandwich spreads and dig right in.

Day 23

"The successful warrior is the average man, with laser-like focus."

- Bruce Lee

Apple Smoothie for breakfast –

What to use:
- Apple (1)
- Cherries (½ cup, pitted)
- Cucumber (1/2)
- Raspberries (½ cup)
- Chia seeds (1 tsp)
- Ice

What to do:
Blitz together 1 apple, ½ cup cherries, ½ cucumber, ½ cup raspberries, 1 tsp chia seeds, and some ice cubes. Pour into your favorite glass and enjoy the apple smoothie.

Borscht for lunch –

What to use:
- Beetroots (4)
- Oil
- Celery (3 stalks, chopped)
- Carrots (2 chopped)
- Mushrooms (1 cup)
- Leeks (3)
- Water

What to do:
Cook and peel beetroots. Grate half of it and thinly slice the remaining. In a large pan, heat oil, and add chopped celery, carrots, mushrooms, leeks and some water. Bring to a boil; add the grated beets, reduce the heat and simmer for about 10 minutes. In another pan, take some more water and boil the sliced beets and simmer on a medium heat for not more than 10 minutes. Drain out the beetroot slices (which you can discard) and pour the beetroot-infused juice into the other

simmering veggie mixture. Remove from heat. Season with spices of your choice and your yummy borscht is ready.

Vegan prawns and some salad for dinner –
What to use:
- Mock prawns (prepackaged)
- Soy sauce (1 tsp.)
- Raw vegetables of choice (3 cups)
- Dressing or sauce of choice (to taste)

What to do:

In a hot skillet, fry the mock prawns with some oil. Sprinkle soy sauce over the mock prawn. Serve hot with crunchy veggies, tossed with a dressing of your choice.

Chapter 6: Meal Plan and Recipes for Block IV

Day 24

"Be miserable. Or motivate yourself. Whatever has to be done, it's always your choice."

- *Wayne Dyer*

Blueberries smoothie for breakfast –

What to use:
- Non-dairy milk (1 ½ cups)
- Oats (2 tbsp)
- Vanilla Protein powder (1 tsp)
- Vanilla extract
- Chia seeds (1 tsp)
- Blueberries (fresh, ½ cup)

What to do:
This needs a little bit of planning the night before. Combine 1 ½ cups of any non-dairy milk, 2 tbsp. of oats, 1 tsp of vanilla protein powder, a little vanilla extract and 1 tsp of chia seeds. Place in the fridge the night before. In the morning, blitz this mixture along with ½ cup blueberries and your smoothie is ready.

Tempeh Cottage Pie for lunch –

What to use:
- Cumin seeds (1 tsp.)
- Onion (1 chopped)
- Garlic (2 cloves minced)
- Capers (2/3 cup)
- Tempeh (1 ½ cups)
- Carrots (2 chopped)
- Tomatoes (1 diced)
- Corn (1 cob)
- Peas (5 oz.)
- Sweet Potato (1)
- Water

- Tomato paste (1 can)
- Salt (1 tsp.)
- Pepper (2 tbsp.)
- Potatoes (2)
- Soy milk (1/3 cup)
- Vegan margarine

What to do:
Fry cumin seeds, onions, garlic, and capers until tender. Put in the tempeh and fry for a couple of minutes more. Add carrots, tomatoes, corn, peas, and sweet potato and cook for another 2-3 minutes. Add water and tomato paste; bring to a boil, reduce heat and simmer until the liquid reduces, but ensure that the mixture does not get too dry. Add salt and pepper for seasoning.

Nicely Mash par-boiled potatoes with soymilk and vegan margarine. Season this with salt and pepper. Pour the tempeh mixture onto a baking tray and evenly spread it out. Spread the mashed potato mixture over this layer and sprinkle paprika over the potatoes. Bake in a medium heated oven for 45 minutes until the potato layer is golden brown.

San Choy Bow for dinner –

What to use:
- Onion (1/2 chopped)
- Garlic (1 clove minced)
- Ginger (1 root grated)
- Chili (1 tsp.)
- Mushrooms (1 cup)
- Vegan mince (1 package)
- Vegetable stock (1 cup)
- Coriander (1 tsp.)
- Soy sauce (2 tsp.)
- Lime juice (2 tbsp.)

What to do:
In a large wok, stir-fry onion, and garlic over a high heat. Add ginger, chili, and mushrooms and continue stir-frying for another 3 minutes. Mix in the vegan mince and stir-fry for some a few more minutes breaking down the lumps in the mince as you go along. Add stock and bring to a boil. Reduce heat and continue to simmer until the stock is fully absorbed. Stir in coriander, soy sauce, and some lime juice. Serve hot on a platter of lettuce leaves.

Day 25

"I believe that the greatest gift you can give to the world and your family is a healthy you."
- *Joyce Meyer*

Raspberry lemon smoothie for breakfast –

What to use:
- Non-dairy milk (1 ½ cups)
- Raspberries (½ cup)
- Oats (2 tbsp)
- Lemon juice (1 tbsp)
- Chia seeds (1 tbsp)
- Almond butter (1 tbsp)
- Lemon zest
- Vanilla extract
- Stevia leaf powder

What to do:
This requires you to prepare the ingredients the night before. Combine 1 ½ cups of non-dairy milk, 1/2 cup of raspberry, 2 tbsp. oats, 1 tbsp. lemon juice, 1 tbsp. of chia seeds, 1 tbsp. of almond butter, a little lemon zest, vanilla extract, and stevia powder. Place in the fridge overnight. In the morning, blitz this mixture in a blender until smooth. Your smoothie is ready

Vegetable curry with rice for lunch –

What to use:
- *Vegetable oil*
- Onions (1 chopped)
- Cumin seeds (2 tsp.)
- Garlic (1 clove minced)
- Potatoes (2)
- Cauliflower (1 head)
- Carrots (3 chopped)
- Mushrooms (1 ½ cups)
- French beans (2 cups)
- Peas (2 cups)
- Curry paste

- Turmeric (1 tsp.)
- Coriander (1 tsp.)
- Salt (2 tbsp.)
- Pepper (1 tbsp.)

What to do:
In a pan, heat some vegetable oil, and fry onions, garlic, and cumin seeds until onions are translucent. Add chopped vegetables including potatoes, cauliflower, carrots, mushrooms, French beans, and peas. Add curry paste, turmeric powder, and coriander powder. Sprinkle a little water and cook until the veggies are tender all the way through. Season the curry with salt and pepper. Serve hot on a layer of steamed rice.

Potato and vegetable salad for dinner –

What to use:
- Potatoes (3 steamed)
- Dijon mustard (1/3 cup)
- Vegan mayo (2/3 cup)
- Carrots (3 grated)
- Onions (1 chopped)

What to do:
Steam potatoes and keep aside. Make a sauce by mixing Dijon mustard and vegan mayonnaise. Cut the potatoes and stir in some grated carrots and finely chopped onions. Stir in the sauce. Mix thoroughly and your salad is ready to be polished off.

Day 26

"To keep the body in good health is a duty...otherwise we shall not be able to keep our mind strong and clear."

- *Buddha*

Blueberry peach smoothie for breakfast –

What to use:
- Peach (1/2)
- Blueberries (1 cup)
- Protein powder (1 scoop)
- Green tea (1 cup)
- Chia seeds (1 tsp)
- Probiotics
- Ice

What to do:
Blend together 1/2 a peach, 1 cup blueberries, 1 scoop protein powder, 1 cup prepared green tea, 1 tsp chia seeds, 1 serving probiotics, and some ice cubes in a blender until smooth. Enjoy your breakfast.

Stuffed tofu turkey for lunch –

What to use:
- Firm tofu (prepackaged)
- Tamari oil (1 tsp.)
- Olive oil (1 tsp.)
- Garlic (1 clove crushed)
- Onions (1 chopped)
- Mushrooms (2 cups)
- Celery (4 stalks)
- Sesame oil (2 tsp.)
- Rosemary
- Thyme
- Sage
- Pepper (2 tbsp)
- Soy sauce (2 tsp.)

- Breadcrumbs (prepackaged)

What to do:
You will need a large amount of firm tofu (about 2 kg). Crumble the firm tofu and add a marinade consisting of tamari oil, olive oil, and 2 cloves of crushed garlic. Stir well and keep aside. Tightly pack this tofu in a cheesecloth-lined colander and place cheesecloth over this too. Place a heavy object on top of this arrangement and let it rest for about an hour.

For the stuffing, fry onions, garlic, mushrooms, and celery in sesame oil. Add rosemary, thyme, dried sage, black pepper, and some soy sauce and cook until the vegetables are soft. Remove from heat. Add some breadcrumbs and mix well.

Remove the heavy object and the cheesecloth from the top of the tofu arrangement. Using a big ladle, scoop out tofu from the top such that about an inch of tofu is left on three sides. Press the stuffing into this hollow and put back the scooped tofu on top and press down firmly on all sides. Turn this over onto a greased baking dish and remove the other cheesecloth too. Bake the stuffed tofu for an hour until the top is nice and brown. Remove from the oven and cool. Your stuffed tofu is ready to be carved.

***Zucchini fritters for dinner* –**

What to use:
- Zucchini (3)
- All-Purpose Flour (2/3 cup)
- Salt (1 tsp.)
- Pepper (2 tbsp.)
- Breadcrumbs (1/3 cup)
- Herbs
- Oil

What to do:
Cut zucchini into baton shapes. Make a batter with all-purpose flour and season this with salt and pepper. Make a mixture of breadcrumbs and herbs. Dip the zucchini into the batter, then coat with the breadcrumb mixture and deep fry in hot oil. Serve hot with any sauce or chutney.

Day 27

"There's nothing more important than our good health- that's our principal capital asset."

- Arlen Specter

Pumpkin banana smoothie for breakfast –

What to use:
- Almond milk (1 cup)
- Banana (1/2)
- Pumpkin (canned, ½ cup)
- Maple syrup (½ tsp)
- Vanilla Extract
- Ginger (ground)
- All Spice
- Ice

What to do:
Blend together 1 cup almond milk, ½ banana, ½ cup canned pumpkin, ½ tsp maple syrup, vanilla extract, a little ground ginger, a pinch of all spice powder, and ice cubes in a food processor. When a thick, smooth consistency is reached, you can gulp down your smoothie.

Spanakopita for lunch –

What to use:
- Onions (1 chopped)
- Garlic (1 clove minced)
- Spinach (2 cups, cooked, chopped)
- Mushroom (1 cup)
- Tofu (5 oz.)
- Pine nuts (1/3 cup, roasted)
- Salt (1 tbsp.)
- Pepper (1 tbsp.)
- Vegan margarine
- Phyllo dough (prepackaged)

What to do:
Make a filling with sautéed onions, garlic, cooked and chopped spinach, mushrooms, tofu, and some roasted pine nuts. Season the filling with salt and pepper. Use this filling to make rolls using ready-made phyllo pastry dough. Place the rolls on a greased baking dish and brush them with melted margarine. Bake for about 15 minutes at 350 degrees or until golden brown. Serve warm with a vegan dip.

Vegan sushi for dinner –

What to use:
- Sushi rice (2 cups)
- Sugar (1 tbsp.)
- Rice vinegar (3 tsp.)
- Nori (seaweed sheet)
- Filling choice (optional)

What to do:
Cook rinsed sushi rice until the water is all absorbed. Stir in sugar and rice vinegar with the cooked rice and mix such that there are no lumps. Keep this aside. On a nori sheet, spread this rice evenly with enough space for any filling too. Other fillings to be considered may be avocado, carrots or cucumbers, julienned and placed to roll with the rice. Ensure you do not fill the nori wrapper too much, as then you would not be able to roll the sheets cleanly. Using a rolling mat, roll the sushi filled nori sheet and then remove the mat and cut into bite-sized pieces.

Day 28

"The foundation of success in life is good health: that is the substratum fortune; it is also the basis of happiness. A person cannot accumulate a fortune very well when he is sick."

- P. T. Barnum

Caramel apple green smoothie for breakfast –

What to use:
- Apple (1 diced, frozen)
- Almond milk (2 cups)
- Spinach (2 cups)
- Peanut butter (2 tbsp)
- Dates (2)
- Cinnamon
- Ice

What to do:
In a blender, put 1 frozen apple (diced), 1 cup almond milk, 2 cups spinach, 2 tbsp. peanut butter, 2 dates, ground cinnamon, and ice cubes and blitz together. Your smoothie is ready.

Asparagus and Mushroom Risotto for lunch –

What to use:
- Stock powder (prepackaged)
- Water
- Onion powder (1 tsp.)
- Mushrooms (1 cup)
- Dried herbs
- Vegan margarine
- Onions (1/2 chopped)
- Olive oil
- Rice (2/3 cup)
- Wine

- Vegetable stock (1 cup)

What to do:
In a large pan, mix water, stock powder, onion powder, mushrooms, and choice of dried herbs. Bring the pan to a boil and then reduce to a simmer. In another pan, melt vegan margarine with a little olive oil on a medium heat. Cook the onions until they are translucent and then add rice and stir continuously. To this rice, add wine and stir again. When the wine is completely gone, spoon in a ladle of vegetable stock. Now add the mushroom mixture. Keep adding stock as it continuously gets absorbed. Repeat this until you get the desired risotto consistency. Serve hot.

Mexican Beans and Baked Potato for dinner –

What to use:
- Potatoes (3)
- Mexican beans (3 cups)

What to do:
Poke potatoes through with a fork and then place in a microwave for about 5 minutes, depending on size, so that it is not cooked through. Then cook in an oven until it is crisp on the outside and soft on the inside. Using pre-bought Mexican beans, heat up in a saucepan. If you would like to make homemade Mexican beans and have time for some extra prep, take pre-soaked pinto beans and season with sauteed garlic, onion and olive oil over medium heat. Add green chili, diced tomatoes, vegetable broth and then water until beans are covered. Bring to low boil, then allow to sit in simmer until beans are tender. Season with a choice of seasonings to personal taste and stir, cooking for a few more minutes until flavors are absorbed. Place the beans over the cooked potatoes and enjoy your meal.

Day 29

"Food is really and truly the most effective medicine."
— Joel Fuhrman

Ultra Green smoothie for breakfast –

What to use:
- Spinach (2 cups)
- Coconut milk (unsweetened, 1 cup)
- Banana (1/2 frozen)
- Avocado (1/2 frozen)
- Hemp seeds (2 tsp)
- Ice

What to do:
In a food processor, place 2 cups spinach, 1 cup unsweetened coconut milk, ½ a frozen banana, ½ a frozen avocado, 2 tsp of hemp seeds, and ice cubes. Blitz all the ingredients together until you get a thick smoothie. Enjoy it.

Vegan pizza for lunch –

What to use:
- Vegan pizza crust (prepackaged)
- Vegan cheese (2 cups)
- Red Bell Pepper (strips)
- Green Bell Pepper (strips)
- Mushrooms (sliced)
- Olives

What to do:
Buy a ready-made vegan pizza crust base and layer it with vegan cheese, thin strips of red Bell Pepper, green Bell Pepper, sliced mushrooms, and olives over a layer of vegan pizza sauce, measured to taste. Bake for about 10-15 minutes.

Lentils, Leek, and Potato Soup for dinner –

What to use:

- Potatoes (2 chopped)
- Leeks (4)
- Red lentils (½ cup)
- Water
- Stock powder (prepackaged)
- Salt (1 tsp.)
- Pepper (2 tbsp.)

What to do:
Take chopped potatoes, leeks, and ½ cup of red lentils along with water and stock powder in a large pan. Bring it to a boil and then simmer on medium heat. Once cooked and cooled, blend in a food processor. Add a little hot water if you want a thinner consistency. Season the soup with salt and pepper.

Day 30

"The finish line is just the beginning of a whole new race."
- *Unknown*

Chocolate and Raspberry smoothie for breakfast –

What to use:
- Almond milk (1 cup)
- Spinach (2 cups)
- Raspberries (1 cup)
- Coconut (shredded, 2 tbsp)
- Cocoa powder (unsweetened, 1 tbsp)
- Ice

What to do:
Blend together 1 cup almond milk, 2 cups spinach, 1 cup raspberries, 2 tbsp. shredded coconut, 1 tbsp. cocoa powder, and some ice cubes in a food processor until you get a smooth consistency. Enjoy your smoothie.

Fried rice for lunch –

What to use:
- Onions (1/2 chopped)
- Fresh, chopped vegetables (2/3 cup)
- Soy sauce (2 tsp.)
- Sweet chili sauce (1 tsp.)
- Rice (2/3 cup)
- Salt (1 tsp.)
- Pepper (2 tbsp.)

What to do:
Heat oil in a large pan and sauté chopped onions. Add finely chopped veggies of your choice, with the recipe generally including cauliflower, French beans, peas, cabbage, and corn kernels. Add a sauce mixture of soy sauce and sweet chili sauce to this, measuring to taste, and cook until the veggies are tender. Add the desired amount of cooked rice and toss and mix thoroughly. Season the fried rice with salt and pepper if needed. Serve hot.

Antipasto Pasta Salad for dinner –

What to use:
- Pasta (1 box)
- Bell Pepper (1)
- Onions (1/2 chopped)
- Carrots (2 chopped)
- Cucumber (1 sliced)
- Kalamata olives (1/3 cup)
- Balsamic vinegar (2 tsp.)
- Additional fresh vegetables

What to do:
Cook choice of pasta as per directions on the packet. Mix together thinly diced Bell Pepper, onions, carrots, cucumber, and kalamata olives with some balsamic vinegar and choice of vegetables such as zucchini and tomato to create your antipasto salsa. Add the cooked pasta and toss all the ingredients together until pasta is well covered. Your salad is ready.

Conclusion – How to Stay Committed

If you are trying to change your lifestyle, it calls for immense commitment and hard work. It is quite easy to fall for loopholes and give up early or even halfway through because you cannot find the energy and motivation to handle the changes. This chapter is dedicated to helping you overcome these negative thoughts and help you stay committed to the vegan cause:

Set yourself easy to achieve targets initially – Setting unachievable targets can put you off as you see yourself as a failure. Take little at a time and be motivated by your small achievements. Slowly you will see setting higher targets and achieve them too.

Keep a journal and food tracker and make diligent notes – Write down everything. From what to eat, how much you have exercised, how difficult the day was in terms of keeping you on track, what were the motivation factors, what were the de-motivation factors, and more! Make note of everything no matter how trivial it may seem. When you are looking back, these notes will come in handy and will help you correct any mistakes.

Interact with people who are also facing these challenges – We are social animals and love the sense of belonging and a sense of identity. When we reach out to people who face the same situations that we face, we find that sense of belonging and the fear that we are the only ones with problems goes away. Moreover, when we interact with other people, ideas and best practices can be exchanged which is good for all concerned.

Remember the process of change is always difficult and painful. But, if we do not take up these challenges we will stagnant which is the beginning of any end. You must steel yourself and work hard for a better tomorrow. When you are feeling low, think of the potential positive results of your endeavors and be motivated by those images and thoughts.

So, pick up the shovel, roll up your sleeves, take a firm stand, and start work immediately and be rest assured that you will find happiness, contentment and an amazing sense of achievement at the end of this seemingly arduous journey.

You're fully committed- what's next?

You made it through your 30-day course! It took a lot of discipline and willpower, but you made it like a champion and are now feeling better than ever. Your energy is high, your mind is clear and you are raring to go- and to continue on with a healthy Vegan lifestyle! So, what's the next step? This section is here to give you a few kick-start ideas on how to keep up with the Vegan diet and enhance the healthy new you even further.

Future Meal Planning

Maybe you want to go on with the Vegan diet but aren't sure where to start, or the set meal plan was really what kept you going. If you enjoyed the recipes and plans in this book, you can go ahead and rotate the meals again! Many of the recipes are customizable with different selections and cover enough days with different types of treats that you won't grow tiresome. If you're adventurous and want to try your hand at creating your own meal plan, start with a simple online search. Blogs and websites are plentiful with great ideas and recipes- your favorite vegan meal may be out there waiting at the tips of your fingers on the keyboard! Then, if you are the extreme adventurist, creating your own recipes might just be a fun new hobby! Now that you are familiar with common foods and structure of a healthy Vegan meal, take some of your favorite elements and flavors and see what you can come up with. You may end up with a couple of hit or miss concoctions, but it will be worth the experience and the chance at creating something awesomely new!

Share the excitement

Did you go on this 30-day challenge alone and just can't keep the excitement of vegan living to yourself any longer? Tell people about it and how much better you feel eating and living healthy! Testimonies go a long way as inspiration for people who are feeling miserable in their current ways. You could even get a circle of friends interested in vegan lifestyle and start a newsletter or a blog to keep yourself involved while giving your group updates on new tasty recipes, tips, and motivation. Sometimes someone just needs a helping hand to get started, and your experience is just what they need! If no one you know seems too keen on the idea of Vegan eating, or if you're not sure you have quite the knowledge and gusto to start up an info group of any sort, search online for a Vegan-related forum or blog to follow yourself. You could earn support and knowledge while meeting new, like-minded people along the way. Win-win!

However you decide to keep involved and fully invested in your new Vegan lifestyle, just remember that that's what it is. A lifestyle that you chose for your health and your energy- an achievement to be proud of. Congratulations, and best regards!

Help me improve this book

While I have never met you, if you made it through this book I know that you are the kind of person that is wanting to get better and is willing to take on tough feedback to get to that point. You and I are cut from the same cloth in that respect. I am always looking to get better and I wish to not just improve myself, but also this book. If you have positive feedback, please take the time to leave a review. It will help other find this book and it can help change a life in the same way that it changed yours. If you have constructive feedback, please also leave a review. It will help me better understand what you, the reader, need to make significant improvements in your life. I will take your feedback and use it to improve this book so that it can become more powerful and beneficial to all those who encounter it.

REMEMBER TO JOIN THE GROUP NOW!

If you have not joined the Mastermind Self Development group yet, now is your time! You will receive videos and articles from top authorities in self development as well as a special group only offers on new books and training programs. There will also be a monthly member only draw that gives you a chance to win any book from your Kindle wish list!

If you sign up through this link http://www.mastermindselfdevelopment.com/specialreport you will also get a special free report on the Wheel of Life. This report will give you a visual look at your current life and then take you through a series of exercises that will help you plan what your perfect life looks like. The workbook does not end there; we then take you through a process to help you plan how to achieve that perfect life. The process is very powerful and has the potential to change your life forever. Join the group now and start to change your life!
http://www.mastermindselfdevelopment.com/specialreport

You will also love these other great titles from Mastermind Self Development!

You will want to check out these other great titles Mastermind Self Development. All available in the Kindle store or you can just click on covers below.

http://mybook.to/positivethink

You can also find these titles by searching them in the Kindle store on Amazon.

Mindfulness

Beginners Guide on How to Shut Off
Your Brain and Stay in the Moment

Free membership into the Mastermind Self Development Group!

For a limited time, you can join the Mastermind Self Development Group for free! You will receive videos and articles from top authorities in self development as well as a special group only offers on new books and training programs. There will also be a monthly member only draw that gives you a chance to win any book from your Kindle wish list!

If you sign up through this link http://www.mastermindselfdevelopment.com/specialreport you will also get a special free report on the Wheel of Life. This report will give you a visual look at your current life and then take you through a series of exercises that will help you plan what your perfect life looks like. The workbook does not end there; we then take you through a process to help you plan how to achieve that perfect life. The process is very powerful and has the potential to change your life forever. Join the group now and start to change your life! http://www.mastermindselfdevelopment.com/specialreport

Table of Contents

Introduction

Chapter 1: The Value of Mindfulness

Chapter 2: Creating the Calm

Chapter 3: Peace in Pandemonium

Chapter 4: The Practical Practice

Chapter 5: Maintaining Mindfulness

Conclusion

Introduction

Thank you and congratulations on purchasing this book! "*Mindfulness:* Beginners Guide on How to Shut Off Your Brain and Stay in the Moment" is a book written specifically for individuals who want to become more mindful, but who have a hard time encouraging their brain to be quiet. While you may feel as though mindfulness is not the technique for you, the truth is that everyone who has mastered mindfulness at one point or another had the exact same difficulty!

This book has been carefully crafted to bring resolutions for all who are struggling to achieve mindfulness in their lives. The wording and instructions are created in an easy-to-understand method that will allow you to understand the simplicity of being mindful, and how you can effortlessly draw it into your own life.

Mindfulness is a highly valuable tool that has the ability to achieve many things in a person's life. Whether you are seeking to add value to each day, eliminate the stress of worrying, or improve your quality of life, you can achieve all of that through mindfulness. In this book, you will be guided on how to achieve mindfulness on an average day, even if you are experiencing a particularly large amount of chaos or stress that may be causing you to feel extra edgy.

It is important to remember that mindfulness is a practice. Once you learn how to be mindful, you will have an easy time re-learning it. You will need to make sure you take the time each day to practice mindfulness, even when you become a master at it. Mindfulness is a balancing act where we are continually practicing our ability to stay in tune. Sometimes, you may notice that you have not been practicing mindfulness in your life. The result may show up as added stress, less mental involvement in day to day life, less clarity on what you are doing from moment to moment, and less quality of time spent with those around you. If you notice this is happening, the best thing you can do is become mindful of the existence of the chaos, and allow yourself to realign with a mindful state and start practicing your techniques again. In this book, you are going to learn exactly how you can do that.

Being mindful may feel difficult, especially for beginners. It is not natural in this day and age to tune out from the rest of the world and narrow in on what is happening in the moment. However, once you understand and implement this valuable technique in your life, you will notice that you feel your stress levels reduce significantly. You will also experience life greater, and with more joy. If you are ready to dive into learning about mindfulness, you are ready to begin chapter one.

Chapter 1: The Value of Mindfulness

Throughout history, a huge number of people have practiced mindfulness. As such, we see it across many religions and many other areas of culture. Mindfulness is a simple practice that, when practiced regularly, allows for humans to stay more focused on the specific task at hand, and resist the temptation to worry about or become absorbed in events of the past or the unpredictable future.

Mindfulness is a relatively simple task to learn once you understand exactly what it is and how you can use it in your daily life. This precious technique has the ability to add value to your life in many ways. Those who practice mindfulness on a regular basis notice increased happiness, greater synchronicity with themselves and the world around them, and even health improvements. Mindfulness truly is a valuable technique that has the ability to offer you a number of different benefits.

Emotional Benefits

Many people report a high number of emotional benefits that come from practicing mindfulness in their daily lives, and it makes sense as to why. Being mindful and staying present in the moment allows for people to experience the greatest benefit of each experience in life. Because of this heightened involvement in the experience, people report a greater result from it. The more involved they are in the moment, mentally, the more they understand about the moment and the more value they gain from it. This is because they are not renting any of their mind space out to unnecessary or irrelevant thoughts or emotions for the present moment. They are taking the time to notice every element of the experience, draw in all that it has to offer, and really take a heightened value from it. Because of this, people report feeling more peaceful, less stressed, happier, and a more genuine sense of joy that comes from being mindful.

Look at the below example to gain a greater understanding as to how mindfulness can change a situation:

Situation 1: *Sally was spending time with her Dad, as they often did on Fridays after school. He liked to pick her up and take her out for her favorite treat: ice cream. Sally loved spending the extra time with her Dad, but he always seemed distant. He would regularly check his watch or his phone, and often didn't listen to what hear her at all. Even though she loved having that one-on-one time, she wished her Dad would stop worrying about his work and pay more attention to her.*

Above, you can see that Sally's Dad was not being mindful. His frequent checking of his watch and his phone signified that he was somewhere else in his mind. Sometimes, he was so distant, he didn't even hear her talking! This can be damaging to relationships with other people and can lead to stress, discomfort, anger, and other unnecessary issues between two people. This is not a good state to be in, especially considering Sally is talking about her own Dad!

Situation 2: *Sally was spending time with her Dad, as they often did on Fridays after school. He liked to pick her up and take her out for her favorite treat: ice cream. Sally loved spending extra time with her Dad. He always gave her all of the attention she needed and wanted during this time. He would talk to her about how her day went, ask her how school was doing, and even offer to help her practice more for the cheerleading team! Sally knew he was a busy man because of his demanding job, so she really appreciated that he took the time to put his work aside and give her his full attention for their time together.*

Above, Sally's Dad was being mindful. He was actively involved in the moment, he was listening to his daughter and engaging in meaningful conversation with her. He put away his phone and stopped checking his watch, and he really gave his daughter the quality time that they both needed. This time would nurture their relationship together, and create a more powerful and meaningful bond between the father and daughter, which is valuable for both of them.

Being mindful has the ability to offer a significant number of emotional benefits. The more mindful you are, the more present you are in the moment. This makes your experiences much more valuable and can help bring you more joy, a greater sense of connection, reduced stress, and greater fulfillment in life.

Health Benefits

Believe it or not, mindfulness does have actual physical health benefits. The more mindful you are in life, the healthier you are going to be. While this phenomenal technique isn't so powerful that it can cure ailments, it does have the ability to prevent and reduce the occurrence of a number of symptoms and diseases. There's a very practical and logical reason as to why, too.

When you are mindful, you are present in the moment. This translates to a number of different benefits that contribute to the increased quality of health that can be drawn from being a mindful person. First, being more present in the moment means that you are less stressed and agitated. Remember all of the emotional benefits you learned about a moment ago? Someone who is in a less stressed and calmer state of mind is much less likely to experience common symptoms and diseases that are born from stress. These include but are not limited to: high blood pressure; headaches; tense muscles; a sore jaw; and even some cardiac ailments. Stress has the ability to cause a number of different diseases in our body. While becoming less stressed isn't the *only* way to prevent or eliminate these ailments and diseases, it is a great way to reduce your risk of getting them to begin with. It can also assist you in eliminating them when used alongside a qualified health plan set out by your health provider.

In addition to allowing you to eliminate or at least reduce symptoms and diseases, mindfulness can also allow you to be more in sync with your body. When this occurs, you will be much more likely to take care of your body in the way it needs to be taken care of.

For example, if you are thirsty, you will drink water. If you are hungry, you will eat. If you are mindful, you are likely going to choose a healthy and fulfilling food option over a sugary-filled quick-fix to your hunger. If you are sleepy, you will go to bed. So on, and so forth. The more mindful you are, the more in sync with your body you will be, and the more likely you will take care of it in a way that keeps it healthy and working optimally. Additionally, if you notice something wrong, you will be able to schedule an appointment with your doctor right away, as opposed to ignoring it for several weeks because you are unaware of it at first.

As you can see, mindfulness has a high number of health benefits, beyond emotional ones. When you are mindful, you reduce your risk of contracting ailments and diseases that can greatly decrease your quality of life, or in extreme cases, kill you. This practice is a wonderful technique to stay in tune with your body, listen to what it needs, and nourish it in ways that allow you to flourish and work in the most optimal way.

Worldly Benefits

If you thought mindfulness only had a benefit on yourself, you were wrong! Mindfulness is a practical and strategic way to benefit the world around you, as well! This amazing technique allows you the opportunity to improve your world through several different ways.

First, when you are mindful, you are much less likely to engage in arguments or conflict with other people. When you do choose to engage in a conflict, you will be much more rational about your approach, and the situation will likely diffuse quickly. If it doesn't, you will recognize that no benefit is being drawn from the experience, and you will remove yourself from the situation. Mindful people are generally much less emotionally charged in a negative format than those who are not mindful. They are more likely to be able to handle anger and stresses strategically, which means that even their "opponent" will end the situation in a more calm and rational way. This may simply diffuse one set of bad emotions, or it could trickle and encourage the other person to go learn about mindfulness and practice being more peaceful and calm in their own lives. You never know!

Additionally, the more we are in sync with the world around us, the more we are going to experience value from the world, and give value to the world. We are more likely to notice people who are struggling, so we can offer help. We are more likely to experience the highest joy we possibly can, which truly is contagious! Many other people who experience your intoxicating joy are going to turn around and experience some of their own as a result!

Finally, people who are mindful are generally a lot more considerate of the Earth itself. They tend to take better care of the world around them through many measures, including but not limited to: recycling, not littering, helping clean up after others, taking care of plants and animals, and more! Doing all of this contributes to the healthy production and growth of the planet, which means that you are assisting it in thriving and maintaining its health!

Being a mindful person adds greater value to life, for the person who is mindful both emotionally and mentally, for the people around them, and for the Earth itself. When people are mindful, they are less stressed and more at peace, they are more engaged with those around them, and they are much more likely to experience greater fulfillment out of their lives. This practice and technique is potentially one of the most valuable ones you could ever teach yourself.

Chapter 2: Creating the Calm

The very first step in becoming more mindful in your life is learning to create the calmness. Or, in other words, learning to relax your mind and let things be. In this chapter, you will learn exactly how you can let go of everything that is stressing you out from your past and your future, and focus strictly on the present moment. This is really the biggest lesson in mindfulness that you need to learn. Once you learn what mindfulness is and how it feels, you will have a much easier time applying it to various situations throughout your life.

Learning to be mindful is truly a process. You are going to start out and probably have a hard time with it at first, and then you are going to continue practicing it until you are a master at it. Once you learn how to become mindful the first time, practicing mindfulness constantly becomes easier every single time you practice it. So, if you ever find you've gone a few days particularly stressed out and lacking mindfulness, you will know exactly what you need to do in order to reclaim your peace through mindfulness.

The first thing is understanding exactly what mindfulness is. Essentially, mindfulness is a form of being present in the moment. It is a time where you prevent yourself from becoming absorbed in thoughts of the past or the perceived future, and you let yourself experience exactly what is materializing right in front of you, right in that moment. So, you are noticing the colors of your surroundings, the smells, the feelings, the tastes if there are any, and the sounds. You really want to enrich as many of your senses with each experience as you possibly can, *and* take the time to actually notice them.

The easiest way to become mindful in a moment is to practice the 5-4-3-2-1 technique. This technique became popular within the last few years for good reason. It is an excellent way to help reclaim your current moment and encourage your mind to focus on what is physically going on around you, rather than straying away into other parts of your mind. In order to practice this method, all you have to do is quietly tell yourself five things you can see, four things you can touch, three things you can hear, two things you can smell and one thing you can taste. This helps you focus on exactly what is happening in the present, and keeps your mind actively paying attention to your current experiences.

You should practice this technique any time you want to become mindful of the moment around you. Observing your experiences with all of your senses is a great way to fully immerse yourself in the present and truly gain all of the value it has to offer. The more you practice this, the easier it will become for you.

You may be wondering when you should use mindfulness. Of course, it's not practical to expect that you are going to be mindful every minute of every day. Even mindfulness masters can't do that, so no matter how long and hard you practice, you are going to experience moments where your mind strays away from you. That is completely normal and absolutely okay. The human brain is a natural wanderer and part of being mindful and experiencing life as fully as possible is recognizing that and giving your brain the permission to do so. The goal is not to have you constantly having to stop your brain from doing what it naturally wants to do. Instead, it's controlling your brain to not wander when the situation warrants for you to be present. When you are working, when you are waking up, when you are eating something new, when you are spending time with people you love, and many other situations are more fully experienced when you practice mindfulness while doing so. However, that's not to say that you can never allow your mind to wander. In this short list below, you will learn more techniques about mindfulness and when you should apply this strategy in your life.

Give Yourself Mind Permission to Wander

Since your mind naturally wants to wander, sometimes the best way to become mindful is to let your mind wander. This may sound counterproductive, but the reality is that it will actually save and enhance your mindfulness practice. When your mind wants to wander and you're consistently having to tell it no, you are not going to be practicing mindfulness because you will instead be having an internal conflict with your mind. Rather than allowing that to go on and then stressing yourself out further, you can simply give yourself permission to let your mind wander. You can let it go for a set period of time, say like five minutes, and then when that time is up, you can gently bring your mind back to the present moment and carry on with your mindfulness practice. This sounds like a paradox, but sometimes being mindful of your desire to let your mind wander is the best way to do it!

Practice Mindfulness During Regular Routines

Often times, our regular routines become mundane and repetitive. We do them so often that we no longer think about what we're doing, we just do it. You may notice this to be the case for many instances in your day and life, for example: brushing your teeth, driving to work, large portions of your work day, coming home from work, making supper, and more. These are all a great time to practice being mindful. When we tend to "check out" for these activities, we can stop feeling present in the moment and start working on autopilot. Not only does this detract from mindfulness, but it can actually lead to your emotional run-down, and sometimes even dangerous situations, such as if you are on mental autopilot while driving to work. These are some of the best times to practice being mindful. You may find that your routine is a lot more fun than you were experiencing, or that there are new and more efficient ways you could be doing things!

Switch It Up!

If you are feeling that your life is too full of routines, another great way to practice mindfulness and really gain a lot of value from it is to switch up your routines! If you always wake up, stretch, go to the bathroom, turn on the coffee pot and then flick on the morning news, then try something else for a change! Wake up, go to the bathroom, set the kettle to boil and make yourself a nice beverage and then drink it on the balcony! You may choose to take a different route to work, walk a different way to your office, sit down in a different way, or do any number of different things to help switch up the pace of things. When you break the routine, you give your mind a bit of a break from the autopilot mode and you encourage it to pay attention by making it interested in what is going on. Sometimes becoming mindful of your routine and during your routines will actually lead you to make changes because you will realize you have been doing unnecessary extras, or that certain things aren't as efficient or effective anymore. Being mindful and giving yourself permission to switch it up is a great way to get your brain active in your daily routines again and give it a break from the regular day-to-day activities that can become boring and mundane.

Practice Mindfulness as Soon as You Wake

When we wake up, many of us don't jump straight out of bed. Even if you do, it is still a great time to practice mindfulness. Since you have been asleep for a while, you have been on somewhat of a mental vacation from your body. During this time, your brain has been wandering for several hours, typically. So, this is a great time to practice mindfulness! See if you can notice the light shining in through the window, the sensation of the blankets or the air on your skin, the sound of the birds or of other people in your home, and any smells and tastes you may notice.

The morning is a great time to practice mindfulness because it allows you to start your day off with being more aware of your surroundings. They say that when we start our day out a certain way, it can make it easier to carry on that task throughout the rest of the day. With that logic, if you are mindfulness first thing in the morning, you will likely find it much easier to be mindful throughout the rest of your day. It is a great way to set the tone, have a positive morning, and really create the perfect setting to allow the rest of your day to be mindful and peaceful.

Short and Sweet Wins the Treat

Remember how you learned that mindfulness isn't something that you are expected to, or even capable of, practicing for every minute of the day? If you struggle with mindfulness, sometimes it's easiest just to be mindful in short bursts. In fact, science has proven that if you are mindful for short periods several times during the day as opposed to one single longer period, you will gain greater benefit from it. With that knowledge, it is a good idea to allow yourself to become present for a few minutes at a time throughout your entire day, instead of expecting yourself to become mindful about everything you do all of the time, or only practicing it once a day for lengthy time frames. Being mindful doesn't have to be a long and hard technique that you put a significant amount of effort into for several hours each day. Instead, draw your mind in when you remember to, and practice doing it more and more each day.

Practice Mindfulness When You're Waiting

When we are waiting for things, we tend to become stressed out, bored, or even agitated. Most humans do not like to wait, which means that this is a great time for you to practice mindfulness! Instead of letting your mind wander down the rabbit hole of negativity that leads you to feel uncomfortable and upset about a situation that you can't control, practice being calm and peaceful. Notice the other people in the lineup, recognize that you're all waiting together, listen to the sounds around you, see what else you can notice about the particular situation. You will be surprised at how enjoyable it can be to stop and observe those around us during these periods where we're forced to wait. You can even do this if you're waiting to be taken off of hold on the phone, when you're waiting for an appointment in a lobby, or at any other time that you find yourself waiting around. It is a great chance to regroup and reframe an otherwise bland, or even stressful activity!

Assign a Reminder Prompt to Help You

Many people find it extremely helpful to associate something with mindfulness and use it as an opportunity to remind themselves to be mindful. There are many ways you may do this in your life, and how you personally choose to do it will be unique to you. However, it can be extremely beneficial to have something that you associate with mindfulness that will prompt you to practice mindfulness throughout your day. Some people choose something simple such as a bracelet or a certain trinket they carry around in their pocket, so that any time they touch, see or notice the item, they are reminded to practice mindfulness. In this day and age, we are also granted with the gift of technology. If you find having a trinket around with you doesn't remind you to stay mindful, you may prefer to set reminders in your phone or switch your phone background to something that will prompt you to practice mindfulness throughout the day. However, you choose to do it, having these prompts are a great way to remember to practice mindfulness and infuse it into your everyday life. Again, you don't have to practice mindfulness constantly, but practicing it in short bursts several times throughout the day is an excellent way to increase the value you gain from mindfulness, emotionally, physically, and otherwise.

Practice Meditation

Meditation is essentially a prolonged practice of mindfulness. Many people love using meditation as a means to infuse an even higher quality of mindfulness into their daily routines. Meditation is an excellent opportunity to objectively explore the thoughts in your mind and guide yourself to a new state of calm. This is especially helpful if you feel that something has been bugging you for a while. Meditation may seem difficult, especially to a beginner, but it is actually quite simple. In order to practice meditation, all you need to do is give yourself a set amount of time, set a timer on your phone if you need to, and then close your eyes and release your control over your mind. Every time you notice your mind has wandered "too far", you can gently practice bringing it back to the center. Some choose to hold an image in their mind, and when their thoughts wander, at any time that they've noticed it's happened, they gently bring their mind back to the thought of the image. You may find that your mind wanders a lot, or that it can be hard to even realize that it has done so. This is completely natural, and you will experience this for the majority of your meditation practices, even when you become a master at it. The best thing you can do is give yourself the permission to practice meditation without judging yourself for how you do so.

The Conclusion

Mindfulness is an ongoing practice that you will learn about as you continue to practice the techniques you have been provided with here. You may realize that it is hard at first, but in time you will get much better at it. Remember, there are going to be times that you struggle with mindfulness, even when you are a master. The best way to keep yourself on the path of mindfulness is to set reminders and encourage yourself to practice mindfulness, especially during mundane and routine activities that we generally set ourselves to "autopilot" for us to complete. You will likely find that the more you practice, the easier it is to remember to do so. Like other skills, mindfulness is one you will master if you practice it often enough. This way, if you ever find that you have gone a prolonged period of time without mindfulness, it will be easy to draw it back into your life and pick up where you left off. This practice is not meant to be a stressful one or one that you worry about having to learn. Instead, it is one that will help you learn more about yourself and the world around you, while in turn providing you with significant benefits related to your health, your emotions, your mental wellbeing, and even the world around you.

Chapter 3: Peace in Pandemonium

There is one specific time when you may want to practice mindfulness, but you are having a difficult time. This is one of the hardest points to master mindfulness, and once you do so, you'll know that you are mindfulness master. The hardest time to practice and maintain mindfulness is when you are experiencing any form of conflict. Whether your conflict is internal with yourself, external with another human, or external with the environment you're in, conflict can create a great difficulty when it comes to practicing mindfulness. Consequently, it is one of the best times to practice mindfulness, as well.

The moment you notice you are in a situation that involves conflict, regardless of what type of conflict, you are going to want to use your learned practice to infuse mindfulness into the situation. This is going to quickly allow you to rationalize your emotions, adjust your action, and likely diffuse the situation quickly. You will enable yourself and that which you are in conflict with the gift of being respected and appreciated as it is, free of judgment. You allow yourself the permission to recognize the situation, honor your discomfort, and respond in such a way that allows all parties to be at peace with the resolution. Mindfulness during conflict is one of the most powerful ways to turn a difficult situation into something easier to manage. You are about to learn exactly how you can practice mindfulness during a difficult or conflicting situation, and how it is going to benefit your life in many ways beyond what simple daily mindfulness can do on its own.

The following acronym "RAIN" is a great skill to practice when you are experiencing conflict. This simple acronym will allow you to regain your mindfulness practice and use it as a means to eliminate the conflict you are currently experiencing. When you practice this, you will likely find that at first that it can be difficult. After you become used to using it, however, you will probably find that it becomes easier, or even second nature whenever you are being faced with conflict. The simplicity of this acronym makes it easy to remember, even during a hard situation, and can help you quickly diffuse the situation at hand.

Recognize the Conflict

The first and most important part of practicing mindfulness during conflict is recognizing that the conflict is occurring. You are likely not going to have the time or desire to practice the 5-4-3-2-1 strategy, as conflict is usually fast and heated. Instead, simply take the time to recognize the conflict. You should then give yourself a moment to become aware of your personal sensations. What are you feeling in your body and in your mind? What emotions are you bringing into this experience that may be making it harder for you to be rational? You may want to form judgments around these thoughts or feelings or try and ignore them because they are unpleasant, but the reality is that you need to recognize them, and the best way to do so is to eliminate judgment and simply just recognize as much as you can.

Once you recognize your thoughts and emotions, as well as physical experiences, it will be easier to give them a label. Often when we are in conflict, the only emotion we feel we are experiencing is anger. Generally, that is not the case. We are instead feeling a number of emotions, or one particularly strong emotion that is uncomfortable and often mislabeled as anger. It could be jealousy, hurt, sadness, worry, or any other number of emotions. Recognizing the exact emotions that you experience will give you the opportunity to address them appropriately. It also gives you an opportunity to have a greater awareness of yourself, and potentially learn some important things about yourself that you may not have learned about otherwise.

Allow Yourself (and Others) To Own Their Opinion

Once you have recognized the situation, your personal sensations and emotions, and the particular underlying emotion or emotions that you are experiencing, you need to practice "allowing". This means that you are just allowing life to be. You allow yourself to have your right to your opinion, and you allow others to do the same. You should allow yourself to have the experience of the negative emotions, even if it hurts, and allow yourself to learn from what the emotions are trying to teach you. A great way to give yourself permission to allow things to happen as they are is to mentally say "yes" to your emotions. Allow yourself to accept your emotions as they are, and allow them to be experienced fully. Doing this is going to give you the opportunity to quickly and completely address the emotions in the situation, rather than bottling them up and drawing them out later at an equally destructive time.

Investigate the Situation

Sometimes when you recognize the situation and allow the emotions to be felt and allow yourself to simply experience life, you will feel the conflict quickly fade. Other times, it may persist. If you are experiencing a type of conflict that is particularly persistent and you are having a hard time managing it, you may want to move on to the step called "investigate". This gives you the ability to further explore the situation and grow from it. The following questions are a great way to help yourself address emotions, especially if you are not sure exactly what you are feeling, as well as address the situation, especially if you are not sure of exactly what has happened:

1. "What is the tone of the experience?" (Negative, neutral, or positive)
2. "What specific event triggered this conflict?"
3. "What about this event made it triggering to me?"
4. "Have there been similar events in the past that triggered me before?"
5. "What is the story that I am telling myself about these particular feelings?"
6. "What is the story that these particular feelings are trying to tell me?"
7. "Are there any alternative stories that exist for these feelings I am experiencing?"

8. "Is the story I am telling myself actually realistic?"
9. "Do I have any bodily sensations connected to this particular experience?"

The more you investigate, the more you are going to learn from the situation. You will often find surprising and interesting answers that help draw you deeper into your own existence and understand why certain things make you feel certain ways, especially if they seem to be a trend. This will allow you to become more mindful of the conflict itself, but will also allow you to become more mindful of you as a person and how you can nurture yourself in a way that will reduce or eliminate these conflicts going forward.

If you are having a hard time discovering the emotional attachments to the conflict, or are unsure as to why they are affecting you, it can be a good idea to address these with a series of investigation questions. This will allow you to gain greater clarity on the situation and respond in a better way in the future.

Non-Identification from the Situation

While this step is not a step that you take action on, it is one that is involved in the conflict-resolution process when using mindfulness. You will know you have successfully used mindfulness in your conflicting situation when you are no longer identifying with the situation. Instead of saying things like "why me?" or "what did I do to deserve this?", you will be in a position where you understand the conflict and recognize it was simply a difficult situation. Your perspective will be shifted, and you will notice that you no longer identify with the situation and that you instead recognize it for what it is, allow it to be, and carry on.

Mindfulness can be particularly hard when you are in a conflicting situation. It can be easy to become immersed in the feelings you are experiencing and feed into them, whether they are ones of sadness, anger, hurt, or other difficult emotions. When we feel these, we tend to ignore *why* and focus more on eliminating them through action. That is why we often associate yelling, screaming, temper tantrums, and other negative elimination actions with these emotions. The more we get stuck in our heads and fail to address the situation in a mindful manner, the deeper it seeds into our bodies and makes it harder for us to respond in any other way. That is why it is crucial that you practice mindfulness, especially during conflicting situations.

Added Health Benefits of Mindfulness During Conflict

As mentioned previously, there are added benefits of practicing mindfulness during conflicting situations. These benefits are largely related to mental health and have a lasting value in our lives. The first way mindfulness during conflict benefits you is that it essentially trains your brain to react in a more peaceful and rational way with certain triggers. This allows your brain to learn new patterns that will make it easier for you to act with mindfulness in future conflicting situations. The more you practice mindfulness during conflict, the easier it will become!

The second way that mindfulness helps during conflict is by allowing you to address your internal experiences related to specific triggers. This gives you the ability to look deeper within' yourself and truly understand why things are difficult for you. The more you practice understanding your conflicts on this deeper level, the more you are going to understand yourself and the greater your mindfulness practice will be. It will also give you the ability to work through residual triggers and make it easier for you to eliminate those triggers altogether, so you won't have to worry about them coming up for you anymore!

You are halfway done!

Congratulations on making it to the halfway point of the journey. Many try and give up long before even getting to this point, so you are to be congratulated on this. You have shown that you are serious about getting better every day. I am also serious about improving my life, and helping others get better along the way. To do this I need your feedback. Click on the link below and take a moment to let me know how this book has helped you. If you feel there is something missing or something you would like to see differently, I would love to know about it. I want to ensure that as you and I improve, this book continues to improve as well. Thank you for taking the time to ensure that we are all getting the most from each other.

Chapter 4: The Practical Practice

Despite what you have already learned, there are many more ways still to practice mindfulness in your life. The more practical the application is, the easier it will be to practice and the more you are going to learn from it. For some people, setting aside time to practice mindfulness every day is simply not something they are willing to do. While it can be beneficial to do so, there are other even more practical ways to infuse mindfulness into your day, should you decide you prefer to do it that way.

In this chapter, we are going to further explore the practicality of mindfulness, and how you can use it in your day to day life. These simple moments in your life are a great time to practice mindfulness and really draw the best value from it that you possibly can. When you are practicing mindfulness, you may wish to start with a very practical application, then gradually increase the amount of time you spend practicing this habit. Whichever way you choose to do it, it is completely up to you!

Be Mindful When You Eat

Many of us are in such a rush that when we eat, we plow through our meals as quickly as we can. The experience of food has been largely lost on us, especially in modern times where fast-paced life and fast-paced food are the norm. One of the best times you can introduce mindfulness into your day is while you are eating. Being mindful when you eat is an incredible way to turn eating into a pleasurable experience. You will learn what exactly you like and what you don't like, you will give yourself the chance to thoroughly taste the foods you are eating, and you will allow yourself the opportunity to truly enjoy the experience of eating. As well, when you are full, you will recognize that and stop eating, which means you will always feel satisfied and fulfilled after a meal, instead of overfull or uncomfortable. Many people who choose to eat mindfully find that they stay away from foods that are distasteful and unhealthy, like fast foods, and start to enjoy more quality foods, as well.

You don't have to reserve mindfulness for the process of eating, alone, either. You can also practice mindfulness when you are cooking. Take time to observe all of the colors and scents coming together, notice the way the food looks as it becomes closer and closer to being completed. The more you invest in being mindful during your eating experience, the more enjoyable eating is going to be. A great reason to practice mindfulness during your meals is that in doing so, you will spend more time paying attention to your body. That way, when you are full, you will finish. You may notice you become full much sooner than you'd previously thought. This is a great way to stay healthy and allow your body the opportunity to take a break once it's done. Many people who eat mindfully find that they no longer gorge themselves on meals and that they enjoy themselves a lot more. Cooking and eating are a great opportunity to practice mindfulness and truly experience the joy and satisfaction that food has to offer when it is appreciated appropriately.

When You're Dwelling On the Past

Virtually everyone spends time thinking about the past, and at one time or another, we've all caught ourselves dwelling on it. The past is something that can be a valuable learning tool, but it can also detract from our present and future if we start to dwell on it. Many people stop using the past as a learning experience and start using it as a punishment to keep themselves from repeating things they did in the past that caused pain in their lives. What this does is harm them every single time they decide to invest more of their valuable time and emotion into this thought. The best thing you can do when this is happening is become mindful.

Being mindful about your past, particularly when you are dwelling on it, means that you will spend time recognizing that it is in the past. Instead of using it as a weapon against yourself or a punishment, you will start to use it as an opportunity to learn and grow. You will recognize why it hurt you, and what has made you cling on to that experience for so long. You will also have the opportunity to learn how you get through difficult times, and how they can assist you with growth. It won't necessarily make it easier to overcome future internal conflicts, but it will definitely give you a blueprint to effectively get there.

While Driving

Many people these days spend a great deal of time in our cars. Unfortunately, a lot of people also become so used to driving that they are no longer mindful of the experience itself. This is why many accidents happen: people become what we like to call "over confident" and they get into an accident. In other words, they became so used to driving that they stopped paying as much attention and respecting the danger that coincides with driving. A great way to change this up is to practice mindfulness while you are driving. When you are driving, you can practice mindfulness by spending more time noticing what is around you, paying attention to your mirrors, and watching your speed. You can take a few deep breaths when you're at stoplights and regroup yourself. Sometimes, a great way to enhance your mindfulness when driving is to turn off the music and really pay attention to the moment around you. This change in the familiar sound that fills your car can really help trigger you to become more mindful. Using time spent driving in your car is a great opportunity to practice mindfulness, as well as eliminate the "overconfidence" factor that can be a major risk when people are too comfortable with their driving patterns and routines.

When You Arrive at Work

So many people arrive at work and immediately become stressed out. In fact, they become stressed out on their way to work. This stress is often not provoked by anything aside from simply arriving at work. For many people, the workplace is an emotional trigger to experience stress or some other uncomfortable emotion. A great opportunity for practicing mindfulness is when you first arrive at work. Take time to notice how you are feeling, and what sort of physical sensations are attached to those feelings. Then, you can also take the time to consider why those feelings occur, and how they are truly affecting your day-to-day life. The reality is, many of us, if not all of us, have to work and keep our jobs. Since that is a factor we cannot change, it is not valuable to allow it to cause us significant stress and internal turmoil each day. Instead, you can address these emotions and practice mindfulness to allow yourself to realistically perceive the experience and draw more enjoyment out of your working experiences.

On Your Work Break

Another great time to ground yourself is when you're taking a break at work. This mindfulness experience allows you to regroup from any stress that your work may have caused up until that point, and then start working again with a new, more peaceful frame of mind. Being mindful at work is very important because this is where many of us tend to draw stress from. The more you are able to become mindful of your experiences, shift your focus and perspective, and learn to enjoy your working experience, the less stressful the workplace is going to become for you. A great way to do this is on your breaks.

Alternatively, if you are having a particularly stressful day, it can be beneficial to take a short unscheduled break to practice mindfulness. You can do this in a simple two-minute trip to the washroom. All you need to do is head into the bathroom, and start practicing your mindfulness. You can use the 5-4-3-2-1 method to ground yourself and keep yourself in the present moment. In the process, it will let you take a second to regroup and shift your focus to something more positive that is associated with your work. This is a great way to relieve sudden and urgent stressors that can arise while we are at work.

It is a really good idea to spend a few minutes out of your work day focusing on mindfulness. This is the perfect opportunity to quickly relieve ourselves from stressful emotions and thoughts and allow ourselves to become present in the moment and remember the bigger picture. Doing this will make your workplace less stressful, and help make arriving at work a more enjoyable experience for you.

Grounding Yourself with Noise

We all hear a lot of noise during the day: phones ringing, doorbells chiming, the sounds of cars going by, and so many other sounds. These are all a great opportunity to practice mindfulness. When you are busy with something, you may notice that these sounds all sort of drop to the background and are no longer something you recognize. You should take the opportunity to recognize these sounds whenever you can, and allow yourself to use them as a prompt to quickly ground yourself. Bring yourself back into the present moment, recognize what is going on around you, and become mindful of your current situation. Most often, this is a great way to alleviate stress and become more present each day. You can use this when you are working, when you are at home, or at any other time during your day when you are preoccupied with your thoughts and want to become more focused on the present moment and the world around you.

Leaving Work

Due to many people working jobs, the workplace truly becomes a great opportunity for practicing mindfulness. Perhaps one of the things that makes this the best place is because it is also the place that most people associate with high-stress levels. This may be because the workplace is a place where we all feel pressure to attend in order to maintain our lifestyles, but many of us are not passionate about our jobs. It can lead to a very mundane, boring, and unhappy experience for many people who are going to work. Even if you don't totally dislike your job or have any particular experiences there that cause you to be able to pinpoint your stress to any one thing, it can still become an unhappy place if you are not inspired by it and passionate about the work you are doing.

Practicing mindfulness is a great way to change that. Since you are already practicing when you arrive and when you are on breaks, it makes sense that another great time to practice mindfulness is when you leave work. Doing this gives you the amazing opportunity of leaving behind the days' stressors and appreciating the current moment. At the moment you leave, you no longer have to worry about work duties until you come back. With that knowledge, you should spend time each day practicing mindfulness and leaving your work stressors behind so you can arrive home with a fresh state of mind. Doing this will make your home time much less stressful and more rejuvenating, making it easier to arrive at work the next time you are scheduled to do so.

Arriving Home from A Day Out

Another excellent time to practice mindfulness is when you arrive back home after being away for some time. You may be away due to work, shopping, a trip away, or any other number of things. Regardless of the reason, this is a great opportunity to practice mindfulness. Take a moment to notice the comfort of your home, the familiar surroundings around you, the people or animals that are there to greet you, and anything else that makes you feel comfortable. Do whatever you can to become even more immersed in the current moment. You may choose to diffuse essential oils, brew yourself a luxurious beverage, turn on some of your favorite music, or do any other number of things that will make the experience more peaceful and comforting. These activities will also help draw your awareness to the present situation, making it even more enjoyable for you.

The more you associate your home with peace, comfort, and calmness, the easier it will be to remain mindful when you are home. This is important because you want your home to be a space that is comfortable and safe for you. You should not feel like you have to compensate for difficult emotions or situations when you are in your home. Instead, it should feel like a sanctuary that allows you the opportunity to relieve yourself of the stressors of the external world, and truly enjoy your present moment.

There are many times that you can practice being mindfulness in practical applications. For some people, these opportunities for practicing mindfulness are the best ones, because they allow you to be the most present without having to go out of your way to do so. You do not have to use prompts or "sit on the sidelines" for any given period of time to be mindful. Instead, you simply allow yourself the chance to become mindful at routine moments and turn it into an enjoyable practice that you look forward to on a daily basis. It should be a chance to regroup and recover from anything that may be drawing your attention out and causing stress in your daily life.

Chapter 5: Maintaining Mindfulness

Mindfulness is something that we must practice, constantly. It is not something we achieve ones and maintain forever. Rather, it is something that we must practice on a daily basis in order to maintain. Knowing this, you may find it sometimes is harder to maintain your state of mindfulness than it is for other times. Allow this to bring you peace, knowing that falling out of tune is completely normal. Additionally, the more you fall out of tune and regain your mindfulness, the easier it will be to regain it in the future.

Sometimes, it may be days or even weeks before you notice that you have fallen out of the routine of mindfulness. When you are brand new to the practice, it is easy to forget that you are working to be more mindful in your life. It is not uncommon for people to be extremely mindful for the first several days, and then just completely forget about it. Or, they may even become worn out. Sometimes, being mindful really forces us to confront emotional triggers that we are not interested in confronting. This can make it feel difficult to maintain and may make you feel like it is more comfortable to be ignorant than it is to be mindful. Realize that it is completely normal to run into these blocks, even for the most mindful people you will ever meet.

There are many ways you can contribute to maintaining your mindfulness, several of which we have already explored and discussed in this book. However, it is important to realize that it won't always be easy to maintain your mindfulness. As you've already learned, when there is chaos or confrontation, or when you are experiencing pandemonium, it can be difficult to maintain your mindfulness.

However, sometimes it's just difficult in general. When you are not already wired to a mindful state, it can be hard to remember to stay mindful. Sometimes, you might struggle to remember to do it, not just during hard times, but at any time, because you are not used to it. You may find that you don't realize you haven't been mindful until after the situation has already passed, and then feel guilty or regretful that you didn't do it differently.

There are several things you should realize and do if this occurs, which will help you maintain a mindful state, even if it's sometimes difficult to remember. Below, we are going to explore the various stages of regaining mindfulness, even when you are forgetful or hardwired to respond to situations in a different way.

Give Yourself Permission to Go Slow

Changes don't happen overnight, especially when you are talking about changes for things that you have been doing for many years, perhaps even your whole life. There are no magic formulas, genies or spells that you can use to help you instantaneously become a more mindful person. Instead, you will have to work towards being mindful every day of your life, even once you've already mastered the art of mindfulness.

It is important that you give yourself permission to go as slow as you need to. You are not going to be able to respond to every single situation with mindfulness just because you've decided that's what you want to do. Instead, you are going to find that you will actually rarely respond with mindfulness at first, and that may be very frustrating for you. Realize that you will need to take your time and respect your need to go slow and take this as a learning process. The changes that last the longest are the ones that can take the longest to create. The more effort you have to put in to get yourself into a changed state of mind, the more likely that state will last you. Even if you have to maintain it.

It may take you several weeks, maybe even months to become mindful. Some people even take years to master it. You never know how long it will take you, because of all of the different elements that go into being mindful. Your unique blocks and resistances, lifestyle, and existing level of mindfulness, plus many other things will all contribute to how quickly you can become mindful the majority of the time.

Start Recognizing Triggers

The very first step to switching over to *mindfulness* as your new full-time lifestyle is recognizing triggers. If you are having a hard time maintaining your mindfulness practice because of forgetfulness or a later realization that you "could have" responded with mindfulness, it may be because you are not recognizing your triggers. Take some time and start realizing what your triggers are. These will change on a regular basis, just like life does, so you will need to consistently maintain a check-in process where you recognize what your triggers are and learn why they cause you to respond in certain ways. The more you understand this, the easier it will be for you to maintain mindfulness.

It is not beneficial to judge your triggers. Doing this can cause you to create new blocks and resistances which may further drive you away from a mindful state. Instead, you simply want to recognize what they are. This is an opportunity for you to look deeper within yourself and work on it. At first, there is nothing more that you need to do other than to simply recognize these triggers. Remember, changes don't happen overnight. Instead, you are going to need to take your time. Once you recognize these triggers, practice recognizing them in action. Every time a trigger of yours occurs, recognize it has happened and allow yourself to experience it. Don't encourage any changes yet, just recognize these triggers in action. You will need to practice recognizing new triggers every time one occurs in your life, which is why it is such an important step in maintaining your mindfulness practice.

Create Your Ideal Response

Once you recognize your new triggers and are very confident in your ability to become mindful about them as they are actively happening, you are ready to create your ideal response. You may have already been thinking of an ideal response up until now, but now is the time to think of a practical, mindful and realistic response that you could use when these triggers arise. This should represent your ideal method of how you would want to respond to a trigger.

For example, let's imagine that a particular person makes you angry when you are speaking to them. It gets to the point that you no longer have to hear anything from them at all for you to become angry. Rather, you just become angry from seeing them in general! In this instance, it may seem like the person is the trigger. However, it is likely something that this person has done, said or expressed in the past that has created the trigger. This, in turn, led to a situation where every time you see this person, you think about that experience.

Your ideal response may be that every time you see this person, you feel no emotions at all. You don't necessarily need to feel good or better when you see them. You just need to eliminate the uncomfortable and charged emotions, like anger and hurt. Knowing this, you may set the intention that every time you see this person, you will no longer feel emotionally charged. Instead, you will just feel neutral.

The above situation and correlating ideal response system can be applied to virtually any trigger you experience in life. Once you recognize the trigger and understand when it is actively happening, you'll likely start gaining more information about *why* it happens when you are in that specific situation. Knowing that, you can create an ideal response on how you would rather feel and respond to the situation, versus how you are actively responding. Make sure that the ideal response is something realistic and achievable. Setting the bar too high may prevent you from achieving it at all.

Use Your Ideal Response at Least 25% Of The Time

Again, you need to be prepared to move slowly. You cannot expect that just because you have recognized the trigger and set the intention that you will now respond perfectly every single time. That in itself just isn't realistic. Instead, you should be prepared to respond your ideal way at least 25% of the time. This allows you the opportunity to prepare to respond that way, but also gives you immediate permission that if the situation doesn't go as you desire for it to go, it won't be a "failure" on your part. Rather, it is just one of the 75% of instances where mindfulness hasn't taken root yet!

When you notice the trigger, think about your ideal response. The first several times, you may only think about the response and how you may have made it work in that situation. Eventually, you will arrive at a situation where the ideal response feels like it naturally wants to take place from you. This is the time where you can start practicing it. The more you practice it, the easier it will become for you.

It is important to understand that this is a major part of maintaining mindfulness. Sometimes, you may put in all of the effort to eliminate a trigger, only for it to come back again. If you notice a trigger has fully come back to you, you will need to revert back to this step and practice integrating your ideal response. You may even need to adjust your ideal response to be something more appropriate and fitting so that it is easier for you to respond to it.

Realize that this part of the process takes a long time. It may even take you a long time just to get to the 25% mark. Again, give yourself the chance to take as much time as you need, and don't hold judgment for yourself or the situation when you need time. Giving yourself this permission is the best way to make sure that you don't feel as though you are failing, and that you allow yourself to respond in the most comfortable way. Believe it or not, the more you take the pressure off of yourself to act a certain way, the easier it will be for you to act the way you actually want to act. Eventually, it will come extremely naturally.

Practice the 80/20 Rule

Moving to the 80/20 rule is sometimes gradual, but you should keep this rule in mind as your destination point. While it will be difficult to get here right away, eventually this is where you should aim to end up. It is natural that we may experience triggers, even long after we have worked through them and moved on. Sometimes, it's just something that happens. If you can stay mindful at least 80 percent of the time, then you are doing well. More, and you are golden!

Having a rule like the 80/20 rule gives you permission to make mistakes, without having to consider that as a complete failure of your mindfulness practice. It can take off a great deal of stress and pressure, and make it even easier to be mindful the majority of the time. This works even better because it makes you mindful about your mindfulness. That way, on the times you make a mistake, rather than beating yourself up you can take a look at *why* the trigger happened again, and address it. This will give you the best chance of making sure that you can eliminate triggers once and for all.

Watch Deep Rooted Changes Take Place

The longer you practice mindfulness, the deeper it will root itself in your life. Eventually, you will always address things in this method: by recognizing a trigger, addressing it, creating an alternative response, and enforcing that response at least most of the time. Over time, this will be a natural method for you to address virtually everything in your life, and that will ultimately shift you from a life of ignorance towards your troubles and into a life of mindfulness.

Mindfulness is not an overnight practice that can be mastered right away. Instead, you will have to practice and maintain your practice for the rest of your life. It will become much easier in time, but even when you are a master at mindfulness, you may still find there will be times where you struggle to be mindful. This is because life is ever-changing and we are emotionally charged beings that will sometimes react instead of respond.

However, you will notice in time that many deep-rooted and powerful changes take place in your life that will guide you in the direction of mindfulness. As this practice becomes more natural to you, you will realize that you are mindful at least 80% of the time in your entire life. You may not notice the changes as they are occurring, but one day you will look back and see just how far you have come!

Always Journal About It

If you are not one to recognize changes that happen in your own life, a good way to start recognizing them is to journal about it. The more you journal about your experiences, the more you can analyze them and make changes, as well as see how far you have come. Journaling has many great purposes when it comes to maintaining your mindfulness practice.

First off, when you journal you can truly gain a greater insight as to how far you have come. You will start to see exactly where you were when you started, and where you are now. You will likely notice that your ability to make changes become quicker and quicker the longer that you practice your mindfulness strategies, and also that you are more capable of adapting to harder situations.

Additionally, journaling is a great way to identify triggers, understand your blocks, and really gain a deeper insight as to what you are going through. Then, you can make more mindful and realistic approaches to how you will handle the situation and what you will do about it. Sometimes, writing about it can significantly help you alleviate a good portion of the stress that is associated with any given situation. As well, you may notice certain trends that occur in regards to your triggers or emotions and have a greater idea as to how you can increase the peace and positivity in your life through your mindfulness practices.

Journaling is an important part of making major life changes. It allows you to reflect deeper on what you are going through, track your progress, and empty yourself of many thoughts that may be using up extra space in your mind. Then, you can focus on the positive and powerful things you want to focus on, and you don't have to keep them in your mind taking up valuable real estate.

Respect, Love, and Honor Yourself Anyway

Some people who are practicing mindfulness may find it difficult to keep themselves positive and love themselves through the struggles. This is especially true when triggers are particularly emotional, or for those who are really early into their mindfulness practice. It can be easy to feel like you are failing, doing something wrong, or otherwise not having success in your practice. You may also find it easy to punish yourself or drag yourself down for what you are going through. It is important to realize that this is not beneficial and that it can actually detract from your mindfulness practice.

A major part of being mindful is feeling positive about yourself and your life. While this may not come easily to you, it is something you should focus on working towards. If you struggle with mindfulness for these reasons, one of your first missions should be to identify your triggers that get you feeling down on yourself and work through those first. You need to learn to practice respecting, loving and honoring yourself anyway.

There is nothing more detrimental to your mindfulness practice than being out of love and harmony with yourself. This can cause you to sabotage your ability to be mindful because you will tear yourself down every time you make a mistake. That is why it is crucial to give yourself room to make mistakes and to love yourself anyway. The easier you are on yourself and the less you hold yourself in contempt for your mistakes, the easier it will be for you to practice mindfulness in your life. It is very important that you give yourself space and permission to make mistakes, and that you love yourself anyway. This will allow you to be the most successful you can possibly be in your mindfulness practice.

As you can see, it won't always be easy to be mindful. Especially when you are brand new to the practice. Sometimes, it won't necessarily be chaos or difficult times that make it hard for you to be mindful. Sometimes, you will simply have a hard time remembering to practice this new way of life due to you being used to living life in a different way for so long. The best thing you can do is give yourself time and space, and draw yourself back to your practice whenever you realize you've strayed away. It may take a while to get there, but the more you practice, the more naturally it will come to you and the more successful you will be in your mindfulness.

Conclusion

Mindfulness is a powerful practice that has the ability to change your life in incredible ways. When you are mindful, you may experience better health, better emotional balances, and lower stress levels. You will give yourself the opportunity to relieve yourself from symptoms of stress. You also gain the ability to recognize what causes you discomfort, and practice working through it so that you can avoid experiencing those unpleasant experiences in the future. Of course, conflict cannot be eliminated, but you allow yourself to grow as a person and work through these conflicts more easily.

The practice of mindfulness can be done anywhere: in your car, at work, at home, or even when you're standing in line at the grocery store. You do not have to limit your practice to any one place or experience. As well, you do not need several minutes or hours to devote to a practice of mindfulness. Instead, you can practice it in as little as two minutes, if that is all you have to dedicate. In fact, it is better to practice mindfulness for a short period of times several times over the course of the day than it is to practice one long burst and never do it again for the rest of the day.

I hope that you learned how to use mindfulness in your daily habits and that it will greatly help you in achieving a more peaceful and empowered life. The practical methods in this book were shared in order to teach you how mindfulness works and exactly how you can work it into your busy routine.

If you enjoyed this book, I ask that you please take the time to rate it on Amazon Kindle. Your honest review would be greatly appreciated.

Thank you, and enjoy your mindful life!

Help me improve this book

While I have never met you, if you made it through this book I know that you are the kind of person that is wanting to get better and is willing to take on tough feedback to get to that point. You and I are cut from the same cloth in that respect. I am always looking to get better and I wish to not just improve myself, but also this book. If you have positive feedback, please take the time to leave a review. It will help other find this book and it can help change a life in the same way that it changed yours. If you have constructive feedback, please also leave a review. It will help me better understand what you, the reader, need to make significant improvements in your life. I will take your feedback and use it to improve this book so that it can become more powerful and beneficial to all those who encounter it.

REMEMBER TO JOIN THE GROUP NOW!

If you have not joined the Mastermind Self Development group yet, now is your time! You will receive videos and articles from top authorities in self development as well as a special group only offers on new books and training programs. There will also be a monthly member only draw that gives you a chance to win any book from your Kindle wish list!

If you sign up through this link http://www.mastermindselfdevelopment.com/specialreport you will also get a special free report on the Wheel of Life. This report will give you a visual look at your current life and then take you through a series of exercises that will help you plan what your perfect life looks like. The workbook does not end there; we then take you through a process to help you plan how to achieve that perfect life. The process is very powerful and has the potential to change your life forever. Join the group now and start to change your life!
http://www.mastermindselfdevelopment.com/specialreport

You will also love these other great titles from Mastermind Self Development!

You will want to check out these other great titles Mastermind Self Development. All available in the Kindle store or you can just click on covers below.

myBook.to/learnspanish

You can also find these titles by searching them in the Kindle store on Amazon.

www.ingramcontent.com/pod-product-compliance
Lightning Source LLC
Chambersburg PA
CBHW081403070526
44583CB00020B/2652